Negotiating
the Gray Maze

Negotiating the Gray Maze

The Business of Medicine in Japan

Mark A. Colby and Michael P. Birt

FLOATING
WORLD
EDITIONS

Copyright © 1997 by Mark A. Colby and Michael P. Birt.

First edition, 1998

Cover illustration by H. Ishioka and M. Colby.
Book and cover design by D.S. Noble.

Published by Floating World Editions, Ltd.
Printed in the U.S.A.

ISBN 1-891640-00-3

This book is dedicated to Japanese health care providers,
who work long, hard hours under trying conditions.

CONTENTS

PREFACE

Japan's medical achievements over the past century have been enormous. Today's Japan enjoys the world's best longevity rates for both males and females, the world's lowest infant mortality rates, and comprehensive cancer screening programs that reach virtually every citizen. Indeed, Japan's foremost medical challenge—the rapid aging of its society and its attendant problems of chronic disease and dramatically escalating health care costs—is an eloquent testament to the very success of its medical system.

That said, Japan's health care system faces a life-threatening crisis. Virtually no member of the health care profession or individual living in Japan can ignore the tidal wave of dangerous symptoms threatening the health-care system today. Scandal after scandal has rocked the Ministry of Health and Welfare and Japan's medical establishment. Escalating costs and lowered reimbursements have squeezed all health care providers. Even Japan's "big bosses," the men who call the shots, have become targets. Excellent patient care continues, but the coming health care crisis casts a dark shadow. The potential tragedy is that while the crisis is seen by many in government, business, and the health care professions, little is being done to deal honestly and directly with the crisis.

Our goal is to blend two messages: First, the health care crisis is coming and, second, foreign health care companies need to do a better job of learning how to work within the Japanese system.

Our story chronicles the exploits of a young, idealistic, expatriate manager named John. John works for a large multinational medical device company called Medical Technologies, Inc., or MTI, and is posted to Japan as their general manager. Unlike most managers who come to Japan, John arrives with more than the usual vague notions and generalizations about how business is done in Japan due to his earlier stint in Japan. Like most expatriates, though, John's feelings and understanding of Japan follow a common trajectory that begins with idealistic zeal, moving next to confusion, despair, disillusionment, followed by (for those who stay long enough and work hard enough), understanding, patience, and effectiveness.

In the first part of the book, we trace John's initial experiences in Japan as he learns the hard way about Japan's medical industry and health care system. He makes virtually every mistake possible, but in the process he learns valuable lessons about science, business, medicine, and the business of medicine in Japan. He gains an in-depth knowledge of Japan's distribution and regulatory systems. With monotonous regularity, John confronts the confusing but critical cultural component of *tatemae* (outward appearance) vs. *honne* (real intention) in Japan. Through it all John maintains his sense of humor and balance as he deals with doctors, bureaucrats, clinical investigators, manager, and every type of person in the health care system.

Toward the center of the book, John begins to utilize some of his hard-won knowledge in order to shape and build a successful business for MTI in Japan. The key component of his strategy for success is "control." That is, John learns that to be successful in Japan, a foreign company must take control over the various mechanisms and levers that run the business. Rather than simply rely on the assurances of MTI's distribution partner, Morikawa K.K., John learns that he must learn the market first hand. Rather than rely on third parties to control the all important *shonin* (regulatory approval), John learns that MTI must take decisive control of its own destiny. Japan is the second largest medical market in the world and, as such, enormous effort is required to be successful. John's key realization is that what works in the United States may not necessarily work in Japan.

We, the co-authors, want to bring our bias into the open. As foreigners and Americans raised in America, our yardstick for medical care and organization is that of the United States. We both have families who have lived, gotten sick and then gotten better using the Japanese medical system. We both have worked inside the medical community and intimately understand the day-to-day dynamics of the Japanese health care system.

Much of the book is written in a humorous tone. Sometimes we exaggerate to make our point, often at the expense of well-meaning physicians, bureaucrats, and businessmen of all flavors. Our goal is simply to reveal all aspects of the health care system in a way that entertains as well as educates. We fully understand that some people may be offended by our approach and anecdotes. To those people, we implore you to practice tolerance and acknowledge that our intentions are well meant and our methods not mean spirited.

We hope that everyone will both enjoy and learn from our efforts. Experience is certainly no guarantee of wisdom, but this book represents the culmination of more than forty years of shared experience in Japan and the medical industry. Our hope is that future expatriate managers will not need to repeat all of John's mistakes in order to be successful in Japan. In the end, all of us wish to contribute to better health care in Japan and help save lives.

The authors would especially like to thank the following individuals, who offered support and encouragement when others laughed. Thank you to: Jack Arends, George Fields, David Hatton, Jack Huddleston, Stephen LaNeve, P. Reed Maurer, Mark Schreiber, and Leo Tilley.

Negotiating
the Gray Maze

1

December 1996: En Route to Tokyo

His temples throbbed. His face was numb. His chest felt like a jack-hammer was blasting away inside him. There was a surreal quality to everything around, as if sounds were muffled with wet cotton and faces covered by veils of gauze. He looked down at his once-flat stomach, noticing not for the first time the roll that had seemed to have come from nowhere, and shook his head miserably. Basically, he was one sorry guy.

"What's amazing," John thought bitterly, "is that only this morning my entire world was wonderful. I was master of all that I surveyed. Maybe not a master of the universe, but things were pretty damn good."

"Now, I'm left with only devastation. Total defeat. My business is gone. The job I poured twenty-two years of my life into... yanked away. And yanked by someone who knows absolutely nothing about Japan. Just because he's CEO he thinks he knows everything. Good Lord..."

He tried to blot out his image and the echoes of his words with another gulp of Scotch, but nothing seemed to help. Sweat began to bead on his forehead and trickled down the side of his face as he thought back to the meeting. Was it really just this morning? He moaned to himself.

"John, everyone agrees you've done a great job in Japan. But you've gone native. It's almost like you think you own the Japan subsidiary and that you're the only person on earth who can run it."

Expecting to hear kudos for his great numbers last quarter, John was shocked as he listened to Big Ed motor on.

"Your ideas, your plans, everything about the way you do business over there just doesn't jibe with our corporate philosophy. You're out of touch, John. We give you a directive and all you can do is come back with a dozen reasons why you can't implement our plans."

He thought, as Big Ed droned on, that if this guy knew what he'd had to do to succeed in Japan, he'd strew rose petals in his path and welcome him as a conquering hero. Instead, he had to listen to this drivel.

His stomach started to lurch.

"John, you might not believe it, but I know Japan pretty well. I've taken several business trips there and I know how to deal with those people. I'm sure that we can ram through our new corporate global policy pretty much unchanged in Japan. They'll just have to take it or leave it."

What he said next, though, chilled John's to the core.

"It's time for you to come home. We've already picked your replacement for the Japan office."

John was too shocked to do anything but hyperventilate.

Big Ed didn't notice. He punched a button on his desk and said, "Karen, you can come in now." A stylish woman in her thirties strode confidently into the room. Even in his current state of devastation, John noticed that she looked smart in her business suit and heels. That was all John noticed before Big Ed dropped the next bombshell.

"Karen's flying to Japan next week to take over. I want you to spend some time teaching her the ropes before you hand over the reins to her in Japan."

John made some vague gurgling noises, the very beginnings of a protest.

Big Ed raised his hand with an imperial gesture, "I fully understand that it's unusual for a woman to take this kind of position in Japan. But we think it will look good to the analysts and our shareholders. Besides, Karen is well qualified."

Karen immediately took over, "I graduated *summa cum laude* in East Asian Studies at Wellesley College." She was obviously proud of her credentials and supremely confident in her abilities. She continued, "I speak fluent Japanese and have traveled extensively." She was staring at him with beautiful, albeit cool, blue eyes.

John thought a moment, then began speaking to her in slurred, rapid Japanese, "What sort of margins can you give me? I'm getting squeezed by my end-users and I need to keep rice in my bowl so I can keep my men on the job." He used the sort of Japanese a forty-five-year-old male executive working for a distribution company might use—the sort of Japanese that gets spoken after enormous amounts of liquor have been consumed.

Karen stared at him blankly. "I resent this!" she flashed at Big Ed. "I did not come here to be tested." It was pretty obvious that she didn't have a clue what he'd said.

Then, he made a big mistake, a really big one. He showed his amusement at her discomfort.

"Ed," she snapped back, "I told you this self-promoting has-been would never accept me. He made his mind up as soon as I walked through the door. He'll never accept a woman running the Japan office." Karen began shaking her finger at John. "I'm going show this chauvinist bastard who's boss!"

Big Ed was smiling from ear to ear. "Quite a lady, eh?"

John could only stare, open-mouthed at this unfolding scene. He certainly did not consider himself to be prejudiced against women holding executive positions. He'd watched several foreign women cut a wide swath through corporate Japan's "man's world." But the grim reality was that the medical business in Japan was dominated by Neanderthals holding prehistoric ideas on the role of women. Barefoot and pregnant was the ideal feminine state to some of those guys. John couldn't see how it would be in MTI's best interests to send Karen to head the Japan show.

Finally, his mouth began to move again, an attempt at speech. "Ed, this is a joke, right?"

But it was no joke. let go after twenty-two years of faithful service to MTI. No fanfare, not even a gold watch.

He took another gulp of Scotch. He couldn't believe that they would just step in and undo the last ten years of his hard work. Ten years of playing the game in Japan. Ten years of getting slammed in the chops and stepping up for more. Now that he had made a profitable go of things in Japan, this Karen person thought that all she had to do was waltz in and take over the reins.

"Another Scotch, please," he politely asked the flight attendant in business class.

He took a large swallow and his mind floated back ten years. Two marriages ago. A lifetime ago.

Was it really the same flight he was on now? John mused to himself fuzzily. "I was young, energetic and optimistic. And really naive. What was I thinking...?"

Another gulp and he went back in time.

July 1986: En Route to Tokyo

"You know, this is great!" John said to his neighbor in the business class section on United flight 851 from San Francisco to Narita, Japan. "This is the first time I've ever been in business class. Not bad, either. I think I could get used to this."

His neighbor, a fortyish American businessman, balding and twenty pounds overweight, was the inverse image of John, who was broad shouldered and had a distinctively athletic look. He was blessed with deep blue eyes and a rough-chiseled face that seemed to enchant women. The fortyish businessman snorted but John couldn't tell whether it was from self-pity or pity for him. He said, "Frankly, I'd rather be anywhere but on this plane right now. This is my eighth trip so far this year and I can't even count how many times I've made the trip in the past five years. With any luck at all, this will be my last trip over. I shipped the family back home in June and I'm going back to spend a few weeks with my replacement and then I'm outta here."

He looked away, tapped his keyboard and began working again on his laptop PC.

Poor guy, John thought. Either his company had lousy products or he just didn't have what it takes to conquer Japan.

"I can't wait to get back to Japan. And with a dream job! Who would have thought that I'd be coming back as a general manager for Medical

Technologies." He'd come a long way from his days as a missionary in Japan. Well, maybe he *had* oversold himself a bit as a Japan marketing expert. But it couldn't be that hard to set up a company. After all, he was the leading salesman at MTI for seven years running. That plus his five years in marketing were all the tools he'd need, he reassured himself. He could handle it.

Soon his thoughts were wandering to other things, like his first Kirin beer. On his mission he used to sneak behind the bushes for an occasional smoke and beer buzz. A wonderful feeling of independence and confidence swept over him thinking of the golden brew and he began reviewing his ideas on Japanese sales brochures. "We have the best technology in the world," he thought proudly. "Our products will practically sell themselves."

The friendly flight attendant brought a third Kirin, unbidden. She smiled at him and said, "You look nervous. Maybe this will help until we land at Narita."

"Yeah, maybe I'm a little nervous."

"But I'll be OK," he thought, "We've got a good lineup and a good distributor. Besides, people are people and what's successful in America should be a smash in Japan."

The adrenaline eased off and the alcohol kicked in while he watched another tedious airline movie. Before he knew it, the pilot was announcing their approach to Narita.

He was one of the first passengers off the plane and made the long walk to customs, where he stood in the "Aliens" line and watched an unsmiling female customs officer in a blue suit stamp passports.

His alcohol-induced confidence from the flight now seemed like a hazy dream. His flight attendant friend was nowhere to be seen. He was tired, the terminal was overheated by at least ten degrees, he was sweating, and the place was jam-packed with Japanese and their carts stacked high with suitcases.

But customs was a snap. John was waved through; after all, he was just another American business warrior sallying forth to wage battle in Japan. He walked out of the swinging doors to the arrivals lobby, thronged with what appeared to be half the population of Japan. His first temptation was to keep moving toward the taxi line and then he remembered his boss's admonition to keep costs under control. He remembered that Narita was almost sixty miles from the Imperial Hotel where he'd be staying in downtown Tokyo and the cost would be at least several hundred bucks by taxi.

John opted for the shuttle, which he noticed had the intriguing name of Limousine Bus. He bought a ticket and then saw one drive by—it looked just like a bus to him, and certainly not a limousine. He stepped through the automatic doors to wait in the bus line and realized suddenly that July is the rainy season in Japan. He was blasted by a wall of hot, soggy air and a curious combination of smells, some of which he could identify as rotting vegetation, tobacco smoke, and air pollution.

All he wanted to do was sleep. He took his cramped seat on the limousine bus and they lurched off on the eighty-minute drive to the Imperial Hotel. A recorded message in both Japanese and English warned that there might be delays due to traffic congestion.

His neighbor was again an American expatriate in Japan. He had been here three years, he said. John told him he'd just arrived to build MTI into a Japan success story.

He said, "MTI has the world's best technology and a good distributor. We are number one in every market in the world. We're going to take Japan by storm, no question."

His neighbor simply made a noncommittal grunt. "Welcome to Japan." A few minutes later his neighbor began snoring quietly. John envied him his escape. It was dark by now and he stared out the window of the bus. "It sure looks different," he whispered.

There was a fender-bender on the expressway and it took them four hours to get to the Imperial Hotel.

One Month Later...

He woke up with his head pounding and his sinuses felt like they were packed with wet sweat socks. John could blame only himself for the state of his head. He distinctly remembered voluntarily raising his arm to order at least the first five large mugs of beer. After that, inebriation replaced free choice.

But the seared sinuses were definitely not his fault. John didn't smoke any more, but he might just as well have gone through a pack, given the fact that the entire bar was wrapped in a foul veil of smoke. Drinking at a Japanese bar is a carcinogenic crap shoot, with tumor suppresser genes just waiting to be nicked.

The good news, he began to sort out mentally, was that he waking up in his own apartment. After two weeks at the Imperial Hotel, John quickly calculated that his entire annual expense budget was going to be obliterated in a few more weeks. Faced with that ugly prospect, he found himself Tokyo's leading rental agency for *gaijin* (foreigner) apartments, Con Corporation, who immediately sent over a delightful young Japanese woman who spoke impeccable English to show him some "suitable" apartments for a man of his stature in the Tokyo business world.

The bad news, though, was that he was waking up in a small, two-bedroom apartment that was going to cost Medical Technologies, Incorported, the tidy sum of ten thousand dollars a month in rent.

Even worse news was that the "key money," or the sum of various deposits and fees, for this place was almost a hundred grand, and, if he read the contract correctly, MTI would get only part of it back.

Worst of all, though, was that he still hadn't told their CFO, Larry Cullen. Larry, affectionately known in the home office as Attila the Hun for his pillaging of manager budgets, would not respond graciously to this new development. Indeed, he anticipated the corporate equivalent of a cruise missle attack on his Azabu-district bunker. It was going to cost him serious capital back at the home office to cover his ass on this one.

To add insult to injury, last night his neighbor gloated that he was only paying only four thousand dollars a month for his (identical) apartment, and his key money was only twenty thousand. Talk about luck! That nice young woman at Con Corporation had sworn to John that he was paying the "going rate" in Tokyo. Right. John would have to pull every trick in the book to keep Larry from finding out about this little problem.

Guilt, remorse, regret, shame, disgust—all began crowding in on him. His head really began to pound.

"Things can't get any worse." He thought slowly as he staggered the few steps to the bathroom. "Arrgh!" He doubled over. The pain was like a samurai sword slicing deep into his stomach. He dropped to the bathroom floor and the tiles were cool and comforting after the burst of pain. Things *were* getting worse.

"No, not now. Why now?"

He remembered that his doctor warned him at his pre-departure check-up about the possible reoccurrence of his appendicitis. "It must have been all the booze the past couple of weeks," he thought as the pain slowly receded to a manageable level. "Maybe I'll be all right if I just lay here a few more minutes and rest."

After the pain passed, he wandered back to the bedroom. He desperately searched his memory for the name of the cute little thing he brought home last night. "Yuki?" he managed. She stirred from under the covers and looked at him through bloodshot eyes and now-faded blood red lips. Her eyes flickered at the prospect of the tall, red-haired barbarian hunched over in the bathroom doorway. Somehow or other John didn't think there was any lust in that flicker. In fact, he was not even sure there was any recognition, either. *"Byoin e iku,"* he grunted, indicating the now-obvious fact that he needed to get to a hospital—fast.

The taxi driver dropped him off, alone, at the curb in front of Tokyo Metropolitan Hospital. White-gloved and very solicitous after John made a few retching noises in the spotless taxi, his driver assured him that this was the number-one hospital in all of Tokyo and, therefore, all of Japan. John looked up at the gray, nondescript building and felt a growing queasiness.

He looked at his watch, "It's just 9:00 in the morning, I'll beat the rush," he thought as he staggered into the lobby.

The place was jammed. There must have been two thousand people milling around. What were they doing? He was sure that if he could just explain his special circumstances and obvious need that he could cut through the press of bodies.

Thank God he'd had the sense to get his National Health Insurance card just the week before. That, at least, had been simple enough. He'd just dropped by his local ward office, filled out a single form and—bingo—he was insured, for the equivalent of fifty dollars a month (although he did have a co-payment of thirty percent). He wondered what this little experience was going to set him back.

John got in line, fidgeted, waited, balanced on one leg, then another. Every once in awhile the line actually seemed to move. Finally, he got to the clerk and through a combination of bad Japanese, sign language and English words yelled loudly, he thought he had made his complaint understood. The clerk took his form and dropped it at the very back of an impressively thick stack of files that looked remarkably similar to his. Uh-oh. John realized that he had just waited thirty minutes in line to get into the real waiting line.

He figured that he had better call the office. His secretary, the always-cheerful Miss Bamba, was right on top of things. She told him that she'd reschedule his appointments for the day.

"Wait a second," he paused, "I'll be back in the office this afternoon."

"Maybe not John-san," Miss Bamba replied brightly. "I think you will be there most of the day."

"Damn!"

He turned around and looked at a vast expanse of linoleum and row upon row of ugly brown vinyl couches, completely filled with human beings coughing, wheezing and, most amazingly, smoking. If he wasn't sick before, it was just a matter of time now. He could already imagine something viral incubating inside of him. A profound sense of resignation took hold of his soul, as another searing stab of pain grabbed hold of his body.

Just before noon, John heard his name, or at least a close approximation of it, announced and he was sent off to another dilapidated waiting room. This one was also filled with patients, all of whom were separated by very thin curtains. There was an old guy in the next stall, hacking up something pretty viscous. John listened and finally began to wonder whether or not his neighbor would make it until the doctor arrived.

Another thirty minutes passed and then suddenly the curtain parted. A young man—no more than twenty-five—was standing there in a white coat. His doctor and savior had arrived. He looked hastily at the chart and in barely recognizable English, said "What is your problem?"

His first problem, John thought, was that his Japanese was better than this guy's English. His second problem was that the doctor looked as if he was in need of a couple of weeks of R&R in a sanitarium. He looked considerably more than tired. Looking closer, John noticed that the bags under the man's eyes had bags.

John quickly described his previous diagnosis of appendicitis and the intense pain this morning, conveying the information with a combination of Japanese, English and Oscar-winning body language. The doctor made a quick palpate, enough to hurt, smiled wanly and then disappeared. Ninety seconds max.

A not-so-attractive nurse stepped into the room, handed him his chart and told him to go to the lab first, the X-ray department second, and surgery third.

"What? Surgery? You've got to be joking." He grabbed her sleeve. She smiled now and responded in a manner that can only be described as patronizing.

"Everything will be just fine."

In a daze, John staggered down the hallway looking for his first stop, the lab. He found it—maybe it was the long line that clued him to the right spot. He found his place at the end of the line—he was getting pretty good at this line-waiting stuff, he thought grimly. The wait gave him plenty of time to absorb the details of his surroundings. After all, he was in the medical business. But most of what he saw, he didn't recognize. The equipment looked very old and extremely well used—like something out of an old black and white movie. The trouble was, none of the doctors looked like Ben Casey or Dr. Kildare.

Finally, it was his turn. John sat on a chair in front of a large window, one of a dozen spots. The phlebotomist was a kindly-looking lady, who pulled out an old, evil-looking surgical tube and wrapped it around his arm. She skillfully pierced a vein, pulled the blood into a syringe and then slid the needle out with a highly practiced ease. She handed him a small piece of gauze to put on the puncture and John, consumed with self-pity, headed off in search of the skull and cross-bones of radiology.

The X-rays were uneventful. This time the equipment was at least U.S.-made.

Next stop, surgery, for a consult, or so he thought. Once again, he was led into a warren of cubicles with thin curtains. It was nearly 5:00 in the afternoon when an extremely busy-looking physician strutted into his humble little cubicle. He flashed John a smile of sorts and said in passable English, "We're running behind schedule, but we can prep you now."

"P-Prep me now? Prep me for what?" he stuttered.

"To take your appendix out, of course. We need to proceed as soon as possible." he said.

"Can I see the test results?" he asked meekly, thoroughly humiliated and feeling totally out of control.

"They are not here," the doctor said in a brusque tone that left no room for argument. In fact, he looked stunned at John's effrontery.

Even in his current condition, the concept of informed consent bobbed to his consciousness. "What kind of surgeon are you? How many appendectomies have you performed?" The doctor merely grunted. John continued, drumming up his courage. "What's your specialty?"

"Lung, stomach, GI, bladder, kidney... just about everything," the doctor said with a smile. "But my hobby is liver resections," he smiled again.

Talk about a jack of all trades! John was no slouch in the medical field, but this guy seemed to cut anything that moved. "I want a second opinion," he blurted out. A look of annoyance crossed the doctor's face.

"I'm the senior surgeon here," he said with a tone of voice that God must have used when talking with Moses. He scowled and then turned away.

"That's it. I'm outta here." John swung his legs down to the floor and then collapsed on the dirty linoleum as another excruciating dagger of pain cut through his insides. He howled in agony. A few minutes later a very young doctor entered his cubicle. "I am Dr. Mori," he informed John. "I understand that you are going to have your appendix removed." He reached under John's gown and with a practiced hand felt his distended gut. "No doubt about it, it has to come out," as he backed out of the stall.

John realized that he just had his second opinion. He also knew that there was no chance whatsoever of Dr. Mori contradicting his superior.

John barely was aware of the hands that reached beneath him and put him on a gurney. A plastic one, with cracks and tape that partially covered the cracks. With a terrible sense of finality, he knew his time had come. He was going under the knife.

John's Lessons

- Japanese health insurance is available to virtually every Japanese citizen and this coverage is provided at reasonable rates.

- Japanese health care facilities are very crowded, very unattractive and seldom take into account the convenience of the patient. Lino-leum floors and dirty walls are the norm, even for Japan's nationally renowned medical facilities.

- Japanese doctors work very long hours under trying conditions; a caseload of seventy patients a day is not unusual for the average general practitioner. Most Japanese doctors are generalists. Although doctors lay claim to specialties such as oncology or pathology, they seldom undertake the kind of intensive and accredited residency programs which we take for granted in the United States and the West. A Japanese oncologist is basically a surgeon who treats some number of cancer patients. Even formal medical training is abbreviated in Japan. A physician is only required to have six years of post-high school medical training.

- The concept of informed consent, while becoming known, is seldom practiced.

- Japanese doctors enjoy enormous authority and social respect; they operate as virtual demigods. Second opinions are seldom sought by Japanese patients who take the doctor's diagnosis as gospel. Moreover, a young Japanese doctor would contradict the diagnosis or prescribed treatment of an older colleague only at great risk to his career.

- Japan's population is aging rapidly. The Ministry of Health and Welfare (MHW) estimates that one-fourth of all Japanese will be over the age of sixty-five by the year 2020. This stunning fact looms like a dark shadow over all aspects of the health care system today, since the MHW and other Japanese bureaucratic agencies are keenly aware of the costs of maintaining the health of a rapidly aging society.

2

John Goes under the Knife

In a state of abject submission, John felt himself rolled down the hospital corridor towards pre-op. "It'll be over soon," he thought, with equal parts of hope and resignation.

The hope part was definitely premature. His gurney was inserted into a holding pattern in the corridor outside the surgical suite. He was number four in line for takeoff, with the others all seemingly awaiting a similar fate. Half an hour later he wished he had brought something, anything, to break the monotony. Instead, he watched a small spider carefully weave a web in the corner of the dirty, water-stained ceiling.

By 7:30 John figured he had been there for well over an hour. Two of the beds ahead of him had been wheeled through the double doors to their destinations, leaving just him and another passive victim.

At 9:30 he awoke with a jolt as the gurney suddenly burst through the doors into the real pre-op area. It was definitely cleaner than the pre-pre-op, but it still had a funny smell of something not quite right. A very young, very cute nurse told him to take off his clothes and put them into a blue laundry basket. Then she handed him a very skimpy gown which had seen better days.

He continued to lay there for another hour waiting for those wonderful pre-op medications. "A little diazepam would really hit the spot," he thought wistfully. Speaking of hitting the spot, John realized that he had not eaten all day. He was famished.

His cute nurse returned and handed him disinfectant, a sponge and a large bowl. "Dinner?" He joked. She smiled and then instructed him to wash his abdomen for ten minutes. While he was faithfully complying with her instructions, she attached some green reusable suction cups to his chest. He immediately recognized these as Welsh cups, which had been abandoned in the States sometime in the sixties in favor of sterile disposable electrodes for cardiovascular monitoring. He prayed that they'd been sterilized, but he was also pretty sure that the hope was futile, given the steady stream of patients and the general appearance of the hospital. Well, they were just electrodes, anyway.

Finally, it was time for his rendezvous with destiny. They wheeled him into the operating room. "Hey, you forgot my pre-medication." he yelled. He pleaded. Silence was the only response. He was encircled by a large group of people in gowns, all apparently straining to get their first look at the prostrate foreigner with the distended gut. John self-consciously covered his crotch. Out of the corner of his eye, he noticed a somewhat older gentleman releasing something into the IV tube which had just been jammed into his arm a few moments earlier.

He tried to formulate a meaningful and coherent Japanese sentence to the effect of, "What are you doing?" It never got out. His lungs froze and he passed over into the land of darkness.

John Lives and Then Recovers

He woke angry, hungry, in pain, and feeling sorry for himself. As he began to focus on the room around him, John realized that he was in a ward with nine other patients. Maybe "ward" was too flattering a word. Maybe "prison" was better, he thought, noticing the bars on the windows. Every eye in the place was on him as he struggled to sit up in his bed.

"How do you feel?" asked the prisoner to his right. John turned his head and the man beamed a smile at him.

"Leave me alone," John snapped at him. With that sharp display of anger, everyone suddenly became interested in their fingernails.

There was no TV, no radio, no rack of books or magazines, nothing. Out of sheer boredom he began to observe the comings and goings of his fellow inmates. At first, he couldn't quite put his finger on it, on just what seemed to make this so different from any other hospital experience he had had in the States. Then it struck him. This ward of nine people was like a mini-village—an entire community in microcosm. Of course, nurses came in and performed their quotidian tasks and doctors made their rounds, but what really seemed to stand out was how the patients helped each other and the constant presence of family members, who were endlessly coming and going. There didn't seem to be anything like visiting hours in the States. And when they were there, they helped out in ways he had never seen back home, like bringing food, changing sheets and clothing, and so on. When their families weren't there, the patients were engaging each other with constant conversation and games.

Watching this, John began to feel lonely and left out. The staff was no help at all. They were professionals and they did their jobs, but they always seemed harried and on the move. What he realized was that the harmony, or *wa* of the room was the responsibility of the patients, not the hospital. It didn't take a rocket scientist to understand that he had done a pretty good job of upsetting the harmony of his village.

After a day of moping and feeling sorry for himself, he began to come around. He could sit up and it seemed like his operation was a success. Things could be worse, he supposed. His fellow inmates had put a banana and some rice balls next to his bed while he slept. The entire room smiled at him and nodded their heads in unison when he noticed their peace offering. Touched, he smiled back.

That was enough to break the ice. Introductions were made and in short order John was on friendly terms with everyone. The ward community literally seemed to breathe a collective sigh of relief that order had been restored.

His next door neighbor, Abe, became his best friend. In his fifties and distinguished, Abe endured John's vehement tirades against the entire Japanese health system. John told him how angry he was at the impersonal way he was treated. "It was like an assembly line. I felt less than human. No one seemed to care about me as a person."

Abe listened to his comments, always nodding, always providing those crucial *aizuchi*, or verbal cues, the "um"s and "ah"s that tell a speaker that they are being heard, and never contradicting him directly. But when Abe spoke, it was clear that he took exception to John's comments.

"John-san," he quietly said, "You must keep a proper perspective on these things if you are ever going to understand Japan. You call our system impersonal and imperfect. But from my perspective, our system is proof of the postwar miracle and just how far Japan has come in fifty years. When I was a child after the war, Tokyo was rubble from the bombings, everyone was hungry and medical care of any sort was nonexistent."

"Now, every Japanese has access to decent medical care. You're right. It's not luxurious and it may not be the best in the world. But it is adequate and efficient. Personally, I would rather have this system, than one where some get the very best and thirty million have no health insurance at all."

It was obvious that Abe was making a not-so-veiled reference to the United States. Abe was starting to build up a good head of steam. He continued, "I happen to work for a large medical device company here in Tokyo. I understand the economics. We know that we have to make tough decisions—not everyone can have unlimited care and treatments. You Americans are so idealistic and so impatient. You always want the best, now. But your own system is plagued by whining patients and paralyzed by outrageous lawsuits!"

Red-faced from his exertion, Abe gasped, and then summoned his clinching argument, "If our system is so bad, why do Japanese men and women enjoy longevity that is the envy of the world? Why do we have the lowest infant mortality rates? In almost every statistical category of health, Japan ranks at or near the top."

Grudgingly, John gave Abe his due. Intellectually, he could see Abe's line of reasoning and acknowledge its truth. But at a basic emotional level he still could not escape the feeling that too many people and too much individuality was sacrificed to get those good statistics in Japan. "Whew," he thought to himself as Abe closed his eyes to take a nap, "Americans and Japanese are as different as two groups can be."

The next day John's doctor casually informed him that he would have to stay in the hospital another two or three weeks. John went ballistic. So much for cultural understanding. "So help me I'll bust the door down if they don't let me out," he protested.

Later that day, using Abe as his intermediary, they negotiated his sentence down to only two more days.

John left the hospital with a huge bag of drugs, all neatly packaged and beautiful in their many colors, shapes and sizes. The drugs had no names, just indecipherable codes and terse instructions like, "Four times daily."

The doctors attributed his quick recovery to his supposedly strong foreign constitution, compared to the "relatively weak Japanese." He wasn't sure if the guy was kidding or serious. Either way, it was a pretty weird thing to say, John thought.

He stepped outside the hospital and climbed into a taxi. The driver looked like the same guy who had dropped him off five days ago. Same white gloves, anyway. He took a quick glance at a copy of his medical record, which he had finagled by sweet-talking one of the younger nurses. John couldn't make heads or tails of the record, which was handwritten in a Japanese scrawl, but he was going to have it translated and forwarded to his doctor in the States. Just in case.

John's Lessons

- Compared to Western health care facilities, Japanese facilities use far fewer disposables. They perceive disposables as wasteful and very costly. There is even a tendency to reuse disposables in order to reduce costs.

- Sterility is a major problem in many Japanese hospitals. This, when combined with the dramatic over-prescription of antibiotics in Japan, has led to severe problems with sepsis and resistant bacterial strains.

- Taken on its own terms, the Japanese health care system is quite efficient. It uses assembly-line techniques whenever possible and overtly depends on the willingness of the users to accept less than perfect service.

- *Gaman*, or endurance, is a critical component of the patient's experience of the Japanese health care system. Pain and discomfort are an expected and therefore perfectly natural aspect of medical procedures. Moreover, patients are expected to actively contribute to the provision of medical care.

- Community is an intrinsic part of the Japanese health care experience. Hospitals, clinics and all health care facilities expect that fellow patients will maintain harmony and help each other.

- While hospital services are increasingly available, much of the burden of patient upkeep falls on the families. Meals, bathing, and changing of clothes are often duties undertaken by family members.

- Although there are pockets of criticism regarding the health care system and some who demand better service and changes, most Japanese appear to be satisfied with the system and the service they receive.

- Japan boasts the world's best longevity rates and lowest infant mortality rates. Explanations for these statistics range from Japan's racial homogeneity to fanciful theories about longer intestines and different brains. Regardless, the Ministry of Health and Welfare is quick to claim credit.

- The average length of a hospital stay in Japan is three to five times longer than in the United States.

3

John Gets to Work

Anxious to get back to work after his nightmarish firsthand experience with the Japanese health care system, John got up extra early and walked to his office near Shibuya, just inside the Yamanote Line that circles Tokyo.

Miss Bamba was already there. Always cheerful, present, and willing to make the extra effort, she greeted him with a chirpy good morning, "*Ohayo gozaimasu!*"

John responded with a much less cheerful, "*Ohayo.*"

"Bamba-san," he continued, "Please make an appointment for me to visit with Goro-san at Morikawa today."

She responded, "I took some initiative as you have asked me and I called Goro-san. I knew that you would like to get back into things as soon as possible. You have an appointment this morning at 10:30 at their office."

Testing his rehabilitation, John took the subway to Tokyo station; halfway there he promised himself a taxi ride back to the office. After climbing and descending six long flights of stairs and standing on platforms and then the train, he was exhausted by the time he reached the downtown headquarters of Morikawa K.K.

He was impressed with their distributor. They had a very nice building downtown, and over two hundred sales representatives covering all of Japan. They had been MTI's Japan distributor for over ten years now.

"These are such great guys," John thought as he rode the elevator up to the reception area on the sixth floor. "They've wined and dined me at least five times since I got here. Even the president, Morikawa-san, joined us on the first occasion. Since then, though, it seems like Goro-san has had the main responsibility for entertaining me," he thought as he announced himself to the smiling receptionist.

Goro and an entourage of Morikawa people quickly joined him in the lobby. They began bowing immediately, with a steady stream of questions about John's health and hopes for his recovery. He felt embarrassed by their solicitude. Goro had visited him several times in the hospital with flowers and gifts, making him feel as if nothing was too much to ask of him. "In fact," John thought with a twinge of discomfort, bowing once again, "I'm almost beginning to feel a sense of obligation to him—as if I owe him more than I can repay."

It reminded him of one of the famous quotes in his first Japanese reader way back when he was first starting Japanese. The quote was about Confucian obligation and the sense that one can never escape the push and pull of obligation in Japan: "Obligation is higher than the mountains and deeper than the seas."

John laughed to himself back then when he finally translated it and understood the meaning, but now he was beginning to feel some of the weight of that aphorism. He hoped that Morikawa didn't think that his obligation was higher than next quarter's sales results.

The bowing finally stopped and they got down to business. The top item on the agenda was the finalization of arrangements for MTI's booth at the big complex at Makuhari Messe. This was a trade show next month in ChibaPrefecture. Walking in, John had thought this was going to be a slam dunk discussion. After all, how difficult could it be to set up a booth at a trade show?

Three hours later he staggered out of the conference room. He was pretty sure the trade show was going to happen, although some of those double and triple negative Japanese sentences left him wondering just what was going to happen.

As they were walking out the door, Goro handed him a few pages of figures.

"What are these?" John asked.

Goro told him, "John-san, these are the new market research numbers we promised you. I think you will be very pleased. MTI has a thirteen percent market share in Japan."

"Way to go, Goro-san!" he thought. Goro then asked him out to dinner, but John pleaded for a night off. Maybe it was his white pallor, but Goro quickly accepted John's regrets and promised another invitation soon when he felt better. More bows and, finally, the elevator doors closed. Whew.

John cashed in on his promise to himself and waved down one of Tokyo's ubiquitous taxis and headed back to the office. It was great to have a few hours to attack the mountain of paper stacked on his desk. Miss Bamba had arranged everything in nice, tidy piles. But they were very high, tidy piles. After he'd been working awhile, he began to sense something wrong. He couldn't put his finger on it, but he knew that a key fact had slipped by him somewhere.

About seven or so, when John could see the surface of his desk again, he knocked off and headed out to dinner. Even better than a taxi, he promised himself a delight well known by some long-term foreign expatriates in Tokyo: Chinese food. Inexpensive, filling, nutritous, and ubiquitous in Tokyo.

His favorite place was only a block from his apartment. John slid the door open, stepped in and heard the standard welcome of *"Irasshaimase!"* Halfway through an order of noodles and pot-stickers, in mid-slurp, that funny feeling came back to him.

He mused, "Somehow those numbers that Goro-san gave me just don't seem right." He looked up, remembering a statistics course he'd taken on his way to getting an MBA. He pushed his bowl away and grabbed a napkin, starting to scribble.

MTI sales in the USA: $120 million
MTI market share in USA: 18 percent
USA population: 250 million

He knew these numbers by heart—he had helped bring them in. On a second napkin, he put the numbers from Goro's research:

MTI sales in Japan: $2.5 million
MTI market share in Japan: 13 percent

Japan population: 125 million

John put the napkins side-by-side and compared them. "What's wrong here?" He knew that Japan's expenditures on a per capita basis were roughly the same as the United States, if not higher. He knew, too, that MTI's product category had caught on like fire in Japan.

He pulled a calculator from his briefcase and started punching some numbers. If he used the same formula for Japan that he used for the United States he got the a different answer.

MTI market share in Japan: 0.75 percent

John went through the process at least ten more times, but the numbers never changed. "I don't get it. Goro-san said our market share in Japan was thirteen percent."

But the more he thought about it, the more the pieces began to fall into place. Like today, when Goro showed him the layout for the trade show. They had a single booth out in the far corner of a huge auditorium. He couldn't read the names in Japanese, but he noticed that quite a few companies had huge spaces.

"Christ! I'll bet those are our competitors." he blurted out. The construction worker next to him stopped slurping noodles long enough to stare at him for a second or two.

"Less than one percent market share." He mumbled in a strangled voice. "If the boys back at the home office find out about this, heads will roll."

There was no doubt about it. Something was fishy in Tokyo and it wasn't sushi. John needed help.

John Gets Help

The elevator doors closed and John finally allowed himself to start panicking. Nothing like a couple of hours with three McGuernsey & Co. consultants to take your breath away and leave you feeling violated. Thank God at least one of them was a woman.

He couldn't believe it. They took him seriously when he said that, maybe, just maybe, he could offer fifty percent of MTI's shares to cover the fee for the consulting project. All three whipped out their calculators and practically in unison said, "That will just about get us there."

These folks were the worst, but the people at Blake & Co. weren't much better. They were smart, he granted them that. But none of them really understood his product or had a handle on what he needed.

John wanted a company that focused on the Japan medical market, had direct, hands-on experience and really knew how to get things done. Back in the office, John asked Miss Bamba to put her sleuthing skills to work and find him that company.

A few days later, she knocked on his door. He looked up from his desk. He had no empirical proof, but either her legs were getting longer or her skirts were getting shorter. Either way, the impression was entirely pleasant.

She said, "John-san, I think I have found the company you want. Their name is Japan Biomedical Business Development. Their name has popped up several times in my search, and always highly recommended. My friend at the American Embassy suggested that I contact them. Even more important, several of my friends who work at Japanese companies mentioned this JBBD, as it's called. I guess the owners are *gaijin*, like you, but they have a reputation for really getting things done in Japan. I called for a brochure and a client list. Here they are."

John picked up the client list and whistled. "They've got some pretty big names on the list here. But I like the fact that they've got Japanese companies and smaller American companies, too. Maybe they'll let me sit down in their conference room without charging me. Make an appointment for me to visit them as soon as possible."

As soon as possible turned out to be a week later.

He found the offices of JBBD without too much trouble. They occupied a floor in a newer high-rise in the Shibakoen district, near the Russian Embassy and the Tokyo American Club. Not a bad area and close to the entertainment district of Roppongi.

After waiting only a few minutes, John was greeted by an American about his age. Bruce introduced himself and shook John's hand vigorously. Glancing at his business card, John was surprised to see that Bruce was the president of the company.

At first he felt a bit put off by Bruce's manner. He was fairly easy-going, which John liked, but he also had a kind of restless energy underneath that made John feel like rushing.

After the usual pleasantries and a cup of green tea, John began his saga and detailed the whole MTI and Morikawa story. While telling the tale, he couldn't help but notice Bruce's body language. At first, he was nodding his head up and down; halfway through he was going shaking his head from side to side; and by the end, he was doing his best to be polite, but he was definitely smirking and suppressing laughter.

John finished his story and said, "I need some reliable market data. Before I do anything, I need to know what's really going on here with our product and the market in Japan."

Bruce quickly shifted gears. "I'm sorry if I look skeptical. But all I need to do is change the names to protect the innocent and I've heard this same story a thousand times. You many not appreciate it now, but you're actually pretty lucky."

"Lucky?" John retorted. "I suspect our Japanese partner of having systematically deceived us for years and you think we're lucky?"

Bruce explained, "Well, most American medical companies do little more than send a guy over once or twice a year to stay at the Hotel Okura and hoist a few beers with their distributor. MTI thinks enough of the Japan market to send you over and put you on the ground. That alone puts you in the top ten percent."

Bruce continued, "It's amazing to me that people ignore Japan. It's the second largest medical market in the world and approaches the United States in per capita spending on medical products. And yet Western companies spend more time and money building their business in Australia than they do going after the Japan market."

"But Bruce," John interjected, "Japan is such a tough market. There are barriers everywhere and nothing is transparent here. No means yes, and yes means no way."

"Spare me the speech," Bruce responded. "I've heard this countless times. I get so tired of hearing Westerners whine about how tough it is to enter the Japan market. Of course it's tough! Of course there are barriers! And of course things are particularly tough for the newcomer. That's the way the world is. Compare that with what a Japanese or European company has to do to enter the U.S. market. Put yourself in a foreigner's shoes and try to imagine what it's like to deal with the FDA and get a Pre-Market Approval (PMA) for a product."

"If Japanese started whining about the FDA, most Americans would respond, 'Too damn bad,' even though most would agree completely with them. Instead of whining they study, they plan, they throw bodies on the barbed wire, and get the job done. Like I said earlier, MTI is an exception for even putting someone here in Japan."

Bruce and John sat quietly for a few moments while John digested all of this and let the energy level dip down a bit.

Bruce finally broke the silence, "Sorry to sound so cynical. The fact is that this is really a tough problem and there are no easy answers. The one thing I know for sure is that the formula for Japan is that success equals the investment of time, energy, and money. No matter how good their technology is, any company that comes to Japan and hands their product to a distributor and then flies back home is going to get what they put into the relationship. Which is not much."

"OK, OK," John responded. "I get the point. I can't change the past ten years. What can I do now?"

"First of all, you need good, reliable information," Bruce said with an air of authority. "Once we have that information, then we can move ahead to make some good business decisions."

"All I really want is reliable data on our market share here in Japan," John responded. "Actually I want a lot more, but after my experiences with the McGuernsey and Blake folks, I'm afraid that JBBD might start asking for multiple body parts as payment. Let's just keep it to a single limb."

Bruce stared at him and finally said, "That is exactly the attitude that gets people into trouble here. Japan's expensive, but you have to pay if you want to play."

Bruce continued, "It's your money, but here's what I think you should do. You need a complete situation analysis. I want to see all of your product brochures. I want to talk with people in your industry segment. I want to have all the information necessary to put together a real business plan for you and MTI. Otherwise, what's the point?" Bruce began pacing the room nervously, obviously getting worked up.

"I'll work with our folks here and then we'll sit down with you, present the findings and give you a complete Japan 101 seminar."

John gulped and asked the question, "How much is this going to set me back?"

"Normally, we work on a ninety-day project basis, but you need this right away. It'll be fifty thousand U.S. for a report in forty-five days."

He breathed a sigh of relief—Bruce only wanted part of a leg.

Bruce seemed to read his thoughts. "At JBBD our philosophy is to charge a nominal amount for the up-front work—just enough to cover our costs. We want long-term relationships with companies and success fees tied to results. That's where we make our profit."

"Sounds fair to me," John replied. He stood up and shook hands with Bruce. "It's a deal."

On the way to the elevator, Bruce finally asked John the question he had been waiting for and dreading, "What does MTI sell?"

"MTI is the world's leading manufacturer of radio-controlled penile implants."

As expected, Bruce burst out laughing and doubled over as the elevator doors closed.

John's Lessons

- Japanese physicians prescribe large volumes of drugs to their patient, who buy considerably more drugs per capita than do Americans. To understand why, we need only look as far as the reimbursement system in Japan. Doctors in a Japanese clinic are reimbursed for the sale of pharmaceuticals; as much as forty percent of their income derives from the sale of drugs. The MHW is working hard to restrict and eliminate this practice, but it remains stubbornly in place.

- Many Japanese believe that Japanese physiology and biology are measurably and distinctly different from everyone else. They believe that Japanese bodies are unique.

- Japanese business associates regularly provide extravagant entertainment. It is a fundamental part of the business culture. At one level, it provides a demonstration of good will and appreciation for the source of business. At another level, however, it is used as a weapon to disarm and defocus a business partner and to create a sense of obligation and, thus, repayment in the future.

- Reliable market data in Japan is extremely difficult to obtain. There are few dependable public sources and data is hard to gather first-hand. In Japan, a request for data must be made in-person, face-to-face and not by the telephone. Interviews with doctors require weeks of advance planning and abject humility. Many foreign companies mistakenly rely on their business partner or distributor for market data. Knowledge means control and Japanese partners use information to control their foreign partner.

- It bears repeating that Japan is the world's second largest medical market.

- By appointing a distributor in Japan, many foreign companies abdicate their ability to participate directly in the Japan market. Thus they must depend on their partners for access to customer information and the scientific community.

- Japan is a very challenging market. But there are numerous examples of success for Western medical companies in Japan. Perhaps the universal lesson from their success is that results require commitment and investment. Nothing is easy in Japan.

- The very first step towards success is good, reliable information.

4

John Gets a Lawyer

It had been a bad week. John was surrounded by "friends" who all seemed to want exorbitant amounts of money. Even worse, they all seemed to be lying to him.

Now he realized that he had just spent a quarter of his annual marketing budget on hiring a consulting company that, given his present mood, he saw as probably conspiring to cheat him even before the elevator doors opened at the ground floor.

John's only consolation was to remember his real estate agent. Nothing could be worse than a real estate agent.

The phone was ringing as John stepped into his apartment that night. He kicked off his shoes in the entryway and ran for the phone. *"Moshi, moshi,"* John said, almost without thinking using the regular Japanese telephone greeting. Silence. "Hello?" he repeated.

A tentative male voice on the other end responded in English, "Uh, John, is that you?"

"This is John."

"Whew, good! You had me worried there for a second. This is Dr. Haver at the Seattle Medical Center. I hope you haven't had that operation yet."

"Thanks for calling, doc. But I had the operation ten days ago. Why?" he asked, with bile rising in his throat.

"Well, John, we reviewed the test results you sent over and nothing there seems to indicate that you had appendicitis. Your white count was normal. Your amylase was normal. There were no signs of infection of any kind. Basically, surgery was not indicated by your clinical presentation."

Dr. Haver sounded very calm. John tried to stay calm. He thanked him for his call and hung up. Calm quickly turned into blind rage.

"Those bastards!" He fumed. "They must have realized there was nothing wrong with my appendix when they opened me up and saw no inflammation. They just scammed me. My God, what kind of place is this? Well, they're going to pay. They're going to pay good!"

Early the next morning John arrived at his office and repeated a familiar drill with Miss Bamba.

"Bamba-san, I want you to find me the best lawyer in Tokyo. I'm going to sue those bastards at the hospital for taking out my appendix."

"But, John-san, we Japanese really don't sue doctors for malpractice."

"Well, I'm an American and Americans sue doctors who screw up. It's my right and I'm going to exercise it. Someone has to be held responsible. You just find me the best lawyer and leave the rest to me."

A week later John was sitting in another waiting room, quickly thumbing through some glossy Japanese weeklies. A week had done little to take the edge off his anger. A middle-aged Japanese man walked into the room and beckoned to him to follow him back to his office.

Once seated, he introduced himself in good English, "I am Sakota. I understand that you need to see a lawyer immediately."

John was stunned. This guy, his instrument of revenge, looked like he hadn't combed his hair in a couple of days. If suits make the lawyer, this man was a candidate for a Good Will donation. It must have been allergy season—judging by the way the man was sniffling. John tried to imagine this guy standing in front of a jury, pleading his case for a million bucks of malpractice. It was too ugly to contemplate.

But Miss Bamba had assured him that he was the best in Tokyo. So, John carefully laid out his story to Sakota. He listened patiently, as behooves a professional billing at four hundred dollars an hour. By the end, John's heart was racing and his voice was raised as he recalled the indignities he had suffered, not to mention mental and physical anguish. He finished with a flourish, certain that he had enlisted the means to make them both rich.

Sakota's eyes refocused. He blew his nose loudly. Finally, John's lawyer spoke.

"I'm sorry. I can't help you."

"What?" John sat in stunned disbelief.

"I don't know how long you've been here, but in Japan we just don't operate in that sort of fashion. Japan is a non-litigious society. We much prefer to settle these incidents informally. Usually, an apology is enough to settle the issue. Even if I *were* to file a lawsuit on your behalf, it would take ten years to prosecute and the award, even if we won, would not cover your legal costs. Look, you're still alive and walking around. What's the big problem?"

Sakota continued, "If you really feel that bad, just tell the doctors and the hospital. They'll apologize and maybe give you a nice gift, perhaps some money in a formal envelope."

The vein on the right side of John's head was pounding in beat with his heart rate, which was galloping by now. He barely kept his voice below a scream, "But those bastards have to be held accountable!"

Sakota shrugged his shoulders. "Feel free to discuss this with another attorney, but I am certain that you will get the same response. You see, there are very few lawyers in Japan, approximately one-tenth the number per capita as the United States. Therefore, we do not have to stoop to ambulance chasing like American attorneys. Ours is a noble and proud profession. It is one which contributes to social tranquillity, not undermines it."

John watched the man blow his nose again. It was time to leave. Another depressing elevator ride. He walked to the subway station, took the train home and went straight to bed.

John's Lessons

- The number of lawyers in Japan is tightly controlled. A very small percentage of persons pass the annual test to become a lawyer. Many spend up to ten years trying to pass the exam.

- Traditionally, Japanese assuage grievances through gift-giving rather than through litigation. A solatium is always accompanied by an apology. From the Japanese perspective, an apology is the crucial first step towards healing and restoring social harmony.

- Foreign lawyers are not allowed to practice law in Japan, except under very special and limited circumstances.

- The number of medical-related lawsuits is increasing in Japan, but the number remains minuscule compared to that of the West. The same is true of monetary amounts of settlements.

- In 1995, Japanese citizens were given for the first time the right to sue companies with defective products causing personal injury.

- Most Japanese perceive the non-litigiousness of their society in positive terms. But there is a growing demand for at least a modicum of informed consent. Moreover, some Japanese are beginning to acknowledge that the lack of legal recourse means that Japanese physicians lack incentives to avoid mistakes and keep up with the latest techniques as a matter of course.

5

John Learns about Shosha

The next month was a busy time for John. After what seemed like countless meetings and hours of discussion, the plans for the trade show were being implemented by Morikawa and MTI. It was one of the things that struck John as being quite different from the States. In the States, it was easy to get an early buy-off on a project from a group; sometimes all that was needed was for the CEO to say "Go for it!" But as he remembered all too well, often those projects never went anywhere, or they were carefully but methodically sabotaged by the very people who were put in charge. The CEO may have led the charge up the hill, but when he looked around he may have noticed that no one was following.

But Japan was different. While it seemed to take forever to get a project going, the project had a life of its own once the group got behind it. For John, the jury was still out on which was better, but he was beginning to at least recognize the Japanese approach and even appreciate it a bit.

Part of the delay, of course, was that MTI and Morikawa were unveiling a new MTI product in the Japan market and the trade show was the occasion for the launch. John was excited about its prospects. The new MTI product was called the "NeoProbe," a small, subdermal chip placed in the tip of a penile implant to detect changes in a sexual partner's cervix and thus the probability of neoplasm or atypias. John was excited about the NeoProbe's impact on the Japanese market. It was an effective cervical cancer screening device with a total available market of three to four million placements. Now that MTI had its PMA from the FDA for U.S. sales and the time clock for the submission to the MHW was already ticking, John felt he had a chance to really nail the Japan market.

John almost skipped to the JBBD office, he was so pleased with developments in Japan. In fact, he was sorry that he had commissioned the study in the first place. The Morikawa guys had been particularly nice to him lately and he felt guilty at his lack of trust in their numbers and his willingness to doubt a ten-year old partnership.

Once again, Bruce met John in the reception area and again vigorously shook his hand. This time his smile had a slightly amused quality. Bruce said, "I carefully reviewed your product literature and I was impressed. Japan's population is graying steadily and more and more men will be having prostate problems. Your products are obviously going to have a substantial market. Now, I've got those numbers ready."

Bruce led the way into the conference room and they sat down. Without any fanfare, Bruce turned off the lights and said, "Let's get to work. There's a lot to show you." He then pressed a button on a laptop sitting on the conference table and began projecting slides onto the wall screen using an LCD display. Bruce turned to John and said, "This is just the Executive Summary. We have three copies of a 150-page report that provides plenty of detail and data for everything I'm presenting now. I think you'll find it interesting."

Interesting, perhaps, but that probably wouldn't have been the first word that John would have picked. Within five slides John's stomach had begun to jump around. By the end of the presentation it felt like he'd been on a roller coaster.

Bruce turned the lights back on, took a glance at John and then stuck his head out the door of the conference room and called for someone to bring the guest another cup of tea. John finally managed to get a sentence out. "What do you mean, four sales reps? Morikawa has three hundred sales people in the field. It can't be just four."

Bruce replied, "We're sure of the numbers. There's no doubt about them whatsoever."

"Goddamn lying bastards," John mumbled through clenched teeth.

Bruce's answer took John by surprise. "Absolutely not!" He continued, "From their perspective they're telling the truth. What they're doing is counting the sales reps from their dealers and sub-dealers. What you need to understand is that Morikawa K.K. is a *shosha*. There's no perfect word in English to describe a *shosha*, but basically it's a trading company. In this case, with certain lines of domestic distribution."

Bruce stepped up to the white board and began to write some numbers. "There are three tiers of trading companies in Japan, large, medium and small. The big boys used to completely dominate the market until the mid-'80s. The top seven maybe controlled eighty percent of imports into Japan. Some Americans have even heard of them: Itochu, Mitsubishi, Sumitomo, Nissho Iwai... In Japan, they are literally household names."

"The main job of the *shosha* is to help source raw materials for Japanese manufacturing companies and then help the Japanese companies export their products overseas in order to acquire cash and keep the process going. Basically, imports were just something they put into their empty ships on the return home. The critical point is that even the big boys really do not have their own domestic distribution system, even though every Japanese knows their name. As a result, the *shosha* have to "rent" distribution from domestic distributors who are usually small, regional middlemen."

"This is where the notoriously inefficient Japanese distribution system originated. In the medical business, we've uncovered distribution channels that have as many as five or six layers between the manufacturer and the end-user. Each layer takes its margin and time to move the product. You can imagine what this system does to the final end-user price. It's not unusual here in Japan to see the same foreign-made product priced at two or three times the price overseas. Even stranger is to see Japanese products, most famously cameras, that cost fifty-percent less in New York than they do a five-minute walk from the factory in Yokohama."

"So the job of the *shosha* is to get the product to Japan, handle the unpredictable and scary *gaijin,* and translate the technical materials and massage the process. But they're not really the distributor, in the manner that an American thinks of a medical products distributor. *Shosha* get their margins for taking the risk—human, capital and exchange rate, whatever."

"But the world is changing and quickly. Today, increased competition has forced even the largest distributors to consolidate and look for new products overseas. Compared to even five years ago Japan has become much more streamlined, but there's a long way to go. For example, there were arguably eight thousand medical distributors in 1980, while in 1995 the number was below six thousand. To put this in perspective, keep in mind that Japan has the land area of California."

"To bring it down to the business level, one major foreign diagnostics company here in Japan had over four hundred distributors in 1990. Today they have only fifty. They'd love to cut it back even more, but it's very difficult to get into certain accounts unless you have the personal connection to the buyer. That means you have to use that sixty-year old president of a local distribution company to sell to the area's biggest hospital and that means a margin for the guy and one more layer. What's strangest here is that to sell to the hospital across the street, you'll need to use a different distributor."

"This is changing in Japan, but nothing happens fast here. Mergers, consolidations, buyouts are usually the result of the company founder dying and his eldest son either fails to make the grade or just wants out of the business. It is going to take time for that entire generation to move on."

Bruce continued, "Morikawa K.K. is a medium-sized *shosha.* Its main business is exporting auto parts and plastic injection molding equipment. Just a little bit different from high-tech penile implants. The only medical products they sell are MTI's and those of two other companies. For that business, they have four sales reps, two technical specialists and two managers. And one of the managers is *madogiwazoku.*"

John stirred from his shock-induced coma. "What in the world is a *madogiwa?*"

Bruce replied, "It's a slang term that describes someone who stays on the payroll, but isn't given any work to do. Literally, the term means something like "sitter next to the window.'"

John showed signs of snapping out of his comatose state. "Oh great, I'm down to eight people working part-time on my business and now you tell me that one of them is a zombie. Now that you mention it, I'll bet it's Suzuki. They invite him into the meetings, but he never says anything and always seems to just be doodling on his pad. *Madogiwa*, huh? Well, now he's MTI's window-sitter. Why do they do that?"

"Well, there are lots of reasons. Sometimes it's because the worker is incompetent, but it can also be because the worker was on the wrong side of a corporate power play. Maybe he sided with the loser and the winner put him next to the window. In Japan it is very difficult to fire someone and, until recently, it was very tough for a middle-aged executive to move to another Japanese company. So, they hang on until they reach retirement age. Another landing place for *madogiwa* is a foreign company, which thinks it's getting this great employee only to realize, too late, that they got a cast-off."

John had gathered himself enough to summon some pity for these folks. "It must be humiliating to be designated as a *madogiwa* permanently."

Bruce agreed. "You really are like one of the living dead, as you said. You get paid, but you have nothing to do. No job description, and there's nothing you can do to change it. Once you're branded you can't escape the sentence."

John was really beginning to put some stuff together now. "I'll bet the recession has given companies a good opportunity to dump these poor bastards."

"You're absolutely right. We've seen companies where twenty percent were *madogiwa*. In today's competitive situation, a company simply cannot afford to carry that much dead weight. It's been a real shock for these men in their forties to suddenly be outside in the cold. Some of them are so embarrassed after they're let go that they simply don't tell their families. For months, they'll go to coffee shops, movies, anything during the day, just to keep up the fiction that they're still employed."

"Back to Morikawa," Bruce continued. "You need to understand that reality operates on different levels and planes here in Japan. There is one level of polite fiction in which everyone pretends that the situation is acceptable on the surface, but then everyone acts according to a different set of rules. This is called *tatemae* in Japanese. The *tatemae* here is that Morikawa has three hundred sales reps. The reality is that they devote four reps part-time to your business. You may call them cheating, dishonest liars, but they definitely won't see it that way.

"From their perspective, it is your responsibility to understand the system correctly and play the game. After all, you're in Japan, aren't you?"

John took a few moments to gather his thoughts together. For the first time since his arrival in Japan, John was beginning to get a real understanding of his situation. Finally, he said, "You're right. It is different here, or at least different enough that we can't assume that what works in the States is going to be successful here. If MTI and I are going to make the big play here, to hit the home run, we are going to have to play the game and we're going to have to play it by Japanese rules."

John looked at Bruce, took a deep breath and said, "You may laugh at our products, but what MTI sells is worthwhile. I want the Japanese to buy those products. I'll do whatever it takes to win. Just tell me what I have to do."

Bruce smiled and said, "That's music to my ears. Let's get to work."

John's Lessons

- A *shosha* is a Japanese trading company. Older *shosha* typically arose from shipping companies and many have links to the prewar *zaibatsu* (major cartels) and to major Japanese banks. The term *shosha* also refers to smaller and medium-sized trading companies as well.

- Until the early 1980s *shosha* controlled virtually all Japan trade. In fact, up to eighty percent of all imports were controlled by about seven companies. The number of smaller *shosha* have grown sense that time.

- Large *shosha* have been encouraged by the Japanese government as they serve as a control.

- *Shosha* are typically arranged by industry group. In John's case, a medical group has developed a distribution network consisting of from dozens to up to hundreds of distributors. It is not uncommon to have a *shosha* represent the distributor salesmen as their own when dealing with foreign manufacturers.

- The job of a *shosha* is to make a contact with the Western supplier, gain and maintain all import approvals, take initial physical position of the product to be passed immediately to a first-level distributor and take currency-exchange risk (or gain). In the medical industry, it is not uncommon for a *shosha* to mark a product up two to three times before selling to the first-level distributor.

- Intense competition is forcing many large distributors into the role of the *shosha*, but this is the exception, not the rule at this point.

- Many Japanese companies are still operating under the principle of lifetime employment. This has resulted in the practice of shunting useless or politically damaged employees aside by not giving them work to do. They are then referred to as the "sitting-by-the-window tribe," or *madogiwazoku*.

- The Japanese deal on multiple levels when communicating. The most common level is called *tatemae*. This saying or doing the proper, or expected, thing. This contrasts with *honne*, or being straightforward. It is difficult for Japanese to achieve true *honne*, unless they are helplessly drunk, at which point they have an excuse to get down and get *honne*.

6

Bruce and John Plan the OTC Mission

The meeting lasted for several hours. It was 6:30 before Bruce and John wound up the formal presentation and realized that they were alone in the office.

John said, "I'm starving. How about a beer or two and some dinner?"

Bruce cheerfully replied, "Sounds great. I know a good *yakitori* restaurant called Nanbantei in Roppongi about a twenty-minute walk from here. The grilled chicken is great and the beer's cold. You deserve it after what you've been through today."

After they had drained the first glass and gotten refills, John said, "You know, this is one of the best things about being in Japan. Eating and drinking in Tokyo is one of life's great pleasures. But it's not going to last long if I don't start putting some better numbers up on the board."

"I keep coming back to your comment that successful companies in Japan take control of their business, rather than letting their partner do it for them. I can really see now how MTI just kind of gave it all to Morikawa and said, 'It's all yours. Just send us the checks.'"

Bruce replied, "That's the way it looks from this side. To help our clients get a mental handle on the situation here in Japan, I like to use the image of a poker game. At the beginning of the game, when a small American company comes to Japan, the cards are dealt out to both sides. Usually the Western company has only one card, but it's the ace. That card represents the innovative technology that only the Western company possesses. But the Japanese side usually has all the rest of the cards: the card for regulatory approvals, the card for access to the scientific community, the card for access to the end-user and, of course, the most important card for them, which is the money that the small Western company wants and needs. What JBBD works to do is pull some of those cards out of the hand of the Japanese company and put them over on the American side of the table."

Bruce continued, "For example, we help American companies hold the regulatory approvals for their products. We also help the companies connect with the opinion leaders in Japan who are crucial to their success. There are a wide variety of things that a company can do to take control of its destiny in Japan."

"But time and time again, we've seen that success in Japan always begins with commitment. Of course, commitment alone isn't enough—you also have to have good products and service. But without commitment, you might as well pack up your bags and walk home."

They ordered another round of beers and continued their discussion. John said, "I can really see where MTI has not committed to being successful in Japan. Our results have been completely, ah, what was that Japanese phrase you used earlier today to describe our business?"

"*Chuto hanpa*—it means 'half-assed,'" Bruce replied.

"Yeah, half-assed. That sums up our situation here in Japan perfectly." By now, John had completely lost track of the number of beers they had each consumed. It was still a single-digit number, he thought, but every time John tried to calculate it, the room grew noisier, hotter, and smokier. After three attempts he put away his mental calculator, and ordered another round.

"Bruce, if I'm going to get out of Japan alive and my career still on track, I'm going to have to push Morikawa to do a better job for us. But, even more, MTI needs to take control. There's no point in getting revenge. We need results. We need a plan. I kind of like the sound of Operation Take Control, or, OTC, for short. OTC begins tomorrow morning at 9:00 a.m. sharp, when I meet the Morikawa boys. Tomorrow night when we go out drinking, I'll try to get down to the nitty-gritty, or *honne*, as you called it, with Goro-san. But, no matter what, MTI is going to start playing the game in Japan."

At 11:30 they staggered out the door and wound their way through the still-crowded, brightly-lit streets of Roppongi. At the "High Touch Town" intersection in Roppongi, they waved good-bye and John somehow found his way home, firm with resolve to take control of MTI's business in Japan. Tomorrow was another day.

The morning meeting went much as John thought it would. With a straight face, Goro reviewed the numbers that he had given John earlier. Yep, MTI still had a major market share position in Japan. One surprise came when Goro made a passing comment about how Morikawa was being squeezed and would like to negotiate a lower ex-manufacturer's price from MTI to help support them in the tough Japan market. John struggled to keep his face impassive, all the while his mind was racing trying to sort out the information, insights and new perspectives he had recently gained. For one thing, John told himself, he wasn't about to give these guys a lower transfer price as long as he knew they were charging three times the U.S. end-user price. Well there wasn't going to be any more of that high price, low volume game. From now on, MTI was going after market share.

John played it cool throughout the meeting. But there were two or three occasions when John wanted to reach across the table and grab Goro by the necktie and slowly, painfully strangle him. Only two or three, but they were real rib-cage rattlers. Each time, he remembered last night's Operation Take Control, and John knew that his position was still too weak to launch a major counter-offensive. He needed more weapons, more ammunition, more knowledge about the tactical situation before he could launch his first strike. Morikawa still held most of the cards.

His best bet, John thought, was to get to the *honne* level with Goro and see what he could find out. The time to begin was tonight at dinner. Bruce had told him that there was a direct correlation between the number of beers consumed and the level of *honne*. John realized that it was going to be a long night and that his liver was going to take a major pounding.

The Morikawa crew was led by Goro. They went to their usual place in the Ginza, which was surprisingly unassuming on the outside. John was beginning to understand that those were the most expensive places. Dinner was wonderful. Nothing like sea urchin, fish offal, and low tide stuff to hit the spot. The weird thing for John was that he was beginning to crave the stuff. Scary how life here could change you.

John carefully paced himself. But he diligently played the Japanese game of pouring refills for his companions and then toasting *"Kampai!"* to keep the momentum going. Goro was an extremely willing victim in this game. John knew exactly when Goro had reached the point of inebriation, that is, when he told his first joke about MTI's product line.

"Hey, John-san, when is MTI going to come out with its BSD line extension. Get it? Extension." Goro seemed to think that was monumentally funny, as did the other Morikawa boys.

"Jesus wept," John thought to himself. Instead of hitting Goro over the head with a bottle, John instead quietly asked him a question in Japanese, as he poured him another glass of sake. "I was wondering, can I meet some of the salesmen that work for your sub-distributors?"

Goro started coughing violently, with a big gulp of sake halfway down. John gave him a few whacks on the back, maybe just a bit too energetically.

John continued with an air of sublime innocence and complete sincerity, "Of course we both know that all Japanese companies use sub-distributors. I've just assumed that the vast majority of your sales force is that of sub-distributors. Right? Basically, it's rented. Right?"

Goro had recovered enough at this point to respond, "Well, ah, we do use distributors, but we prefer to think of them as our employees, or more accurately, as part of the Morikawa family." From his changed body language, John knew that he had hit the soft spot. Goro was skating on thin ice—he knew that Morikawa had committed themselves verbally and in writing to the effect of having over 250 salesmen.

Goro then launched into a long and very discursive lecture on the rich, complicated culture of Japan. This was not the first time that John had heard a variation of this lecture. He was beginning to recognize this a tactic to stall or obfuscate in an embarrassing situation. Later, John would label this the "Foreigners are Too Simple-Minded to Understand Japan" lecture. John also knew that Goro was struggling to keep the conversation away from the *honne* level as much as humanly possible.

John refused to let him off the hook. "Goro-san, you know that we are good friends, right?" "Yes, yes." Goro enthusiastically replied, lifting his glass in hopes of replacing *honne* with beer. John kept going. "We need to get something straight here. I respect your culture and I ask that you respect mine. May we speak in *honne* terms?" Goro replied, "Of course. I always speak *honne* with you. You are my good friend."

John looked at him and began, "Where I come from, an employee is someone who is paid by a company and works exclusively for that company. Using that definition, how many salesmen does Morikawa have working for MTI and actively promoting our products?"

Goro began to make loud, sucking noises. "That is very difficult to say. You see, in Japan family and company are not distinct concepts. Yes, it is very difficult to say." Difficult to say perhaps, but Goro was finding it very easy to sweat at this point. The other Morikawa men were staring mutely at a fixed point somewhere far, far away.

For the next two hours, John and Goro walked around this subject like a dog circling a fire hydrant to find exactly the right moment to pee. In the end, Goro never gave John a number. John knew that Goro was unable to provide any. If he had done that on his own initiative and his superiors at Morikawa had found out, Goro would have to cut his belly open with a bamboo knife to assume responsibility. No, too many obstacles separated John and Goro from getting to *honne*. There was too much history and too many conflicting motivations for the two of them to set aside the weight of business and culture.

But as the taxi door closed behind him in front of his apartment, John felt that he had made a very important step in Operation Take Control. Just before leaving, he had gotten Goro to promise to take him to meet one of Morikawa's sub-distributors. This, at least, was a promising development. John was one step closer to the elusive end-user in Japan.

John's Lessons

- *Honne* is an elusive commodity in Japan. It is easy to say but difficult for Japanese to achieve. There are also different levels of *honne*. Most Japanese live in a *tatemae* world, only reaching *honne* with a selected few after hours and hours of discussion and being together. Alcohol helps, but it will not compensate for time and commitment toward a common goal.

- The Japanese *shosha* tends to block the manufacturer from having access to the distributors. The distributors typically go to great lengths to block access to the end-users. In many cases they will have favorite distributors and favorite users to run insistent manufacturers through, but the ideal is complete isolation if possible.

7

John Sees Distribution Firsthand

The air was drippingly palpable. A typhoon was approaching Japan, which meant the temperature was hot and humidity was nearing one-hundred percent. Not even the air-conditioner on the train could keep the heat out. On the other hand, Goro and his three compatriots were doing a pretty good imitation of an iceberg. They were definitely less than thrilled about following through on the promise to take John to visit one of Morikawa's sub-distributors. The five of them sat shoulder-to-shoulder, in chilly silence, on the train heading out to the hills of Nagano Prefecture.

The upcoming meeting with the sub-distributor was not the only reason for their frostiness. A few days after the abortive *honne* discussion with Goro, John received a big break. He got a nice letter from a urologist also in Nagano Prefecture. He had a vague recollection of meeting the doctor at the JUA (Japan Urology Association) meeting a few weeks before, when MTI first demonstrated its new radio-controlled penile implant for detecting cervical cancer. Normally, the Morikawa representatives would snap up all of the business cards from visitors to the booth. But this time John happened to speak for a few minutes with the doctor, who had spent some time training in the States, and had kept his card. In his letter, the doctor expressed a high level of interest in MTI's products and requested a meeting with John. After obtaining Goro's promise to allow John closer to the end-user, he didn't see where Goro could complain. So, John accepted the doctor's invitation and set up an appointment.

When John informed Goro of the appointment, the barometric pressure in the room dropped to typhoon levels and Goro began making those sucking sounds again. "John-san, this is entirely out of the ordinary. It is not proper. First, we must ask permission from our sales manager, then ask permission of the distributor and so on in order to arrange the meeting." His Japanese was getting choppy and very fast.

John simply shrugged. "Well, he wrote me and I made the appointment. You have two weeks to make all of the necessary arrangements."

Goro did not give up easily. He spent the better part of an hour trying desperately to convince John that the universe was in imminent danger of another Big Bang unless John recanted. Goro pointed out that he was arranging visits with sub-distributors and end-users through legitimate channels. Wasn't that enough? But John kept the OTC plan in mind and held firm.

In a strained silence they took a taxi from the station, which left them off, sweating, about ten minutes later. The building was the nondescript gray kind you can find in any commercial area in Japan. They walked through the doors, but there was no receptionist. There were boxes everywhere and people rushing to and fro. They announced to a woman at the nearest desk that they would like to see the president of Pinnacle Shoji.

John was ready for the worst. He fully expected a cool reception from the president of Pinnacle, Mr. Takahashi. Instead, he was in for a pleasant surprise. Takahashi practically skipped into the room, shouting orders and instructions to five or six office ladies as he went. John took a handkerchief from his pocket and wiped some sweat from his forehead and sized up Takahashi. What struck him first was his irrepressible energy. He was a five-foot-four ball of energy. Goro had told him earlier that he was sixty years old, but if John had met him on the street he would have pegged him at forty five, at most.

John was even more pleased when Takahashi ignored the Morikawa contingent and directly stuck out his hand to John and shook it vigorously. In passable English he said, "Am I ever glad to meet you." John couldn't help but notice the exchange of glances among the Morikawa representatives as Takahashi led him away to give a tour of his company and facilities. After the tour they headed back to his cramped office for the obligatory cup of green tea. Learning that their meeting with Dr. Tani was not scheduled until the next morning, Takahashi immediately invited John for dinner. Almost as an afterthought, he also invited the Morikawa folks too. Goro and the others had become visibly agitated, something which both Takahashi and John seemed to quietly enjoy with a quick glance at each other.

The mouth of the fish rhythmically opened and closed as they pulled off thinly cut strips of its flesh with their *hashi*, or chopsticks. John was getting used to this sort of thing, even to the point of enjoying it. The restaurant was unpretentious yet comfortable and had numerous middle-aged Japanese women in kimono serving the entirely male clientele. John knew that this signified that Takahashi was reaching deep into his wallet to honor his foreign guest for the evening. Unlike the American host who would surely drop a hint or two about the grand surroundings or the high cost, Takahashi made absolutely no reference to his generosity.

As the combination of good food and plentiful alcohol began to kick in, the conversation between Takahashi and the Morikawa boys grew more animated. John's Japanese was improving rapidly, but he was having great difficulty tracking this conversation because of the speed and the dialect they were using. Obviously, they had had this conversation before. John heard one defiant phrase from Takahashi that he immediately understood, "You guys are making too much money!"

Takahashi turned to John and asked, "John-san, what do you charge for MTIs old radio-controlled size six adjustable implant?"

John was just about to open his mouth to answer when he felt Goro fiercely grip his arm and mutter threateningly, "This is not proper."

John said nothing. He glanced at Takahashi and knew that he knew. The only naive person at the table was John and he was catching on in a hurry. He remembered OTC and kept his peace, preferring to fight another day. Meanwhile, the ping-pong match between Morikawa and Pinnacle Shoji continued. John caught only a fraction of the dialogue, but it was more than enough to convince him that all was not well in the Morikawa Family. John only sensed it at the time, but Takahashi would turn out to be a powerful mentor and valuable ally. He dealt only on the *honne* level and seemed to get away with it. John couldn't figure out how he got away with it, though.

The evening's festivities ended fairly early. John would have loved to spend a couple of hours alone with Takahashi and get the real skinny on the situation. But it was obvious that Goro would never let that happen on this trip. Still, John and Takahashi had a minute together in the men's room, where John offered to reciprocate the hospitality next time Takahashi visited Tokyo. The offer was immediately accepted and John said good-bye very much looking forward to their next meeting, as well as the visit to see Dr. Tani the next day.

John's Lessons

- Distributors in Japan carry out many important functions: 1) Above all, distributors are important because they hold the account with the end-users. Hospitals and clinics only hold accounts with a few distributors; 2) Distributors act as a cash hedge for the hospital or clinic. It is not uncommon for them to hold accounts receivable for net 180 to net 360 days (six to twelve months' worth of stock). Distributor to distributor relationships are, in the minds of the authors, usually but not always wasteful; 3) Distributors call on users as much as often as once a day to fill orders, keep up strong relationships and, of course, gather valuable information.

- Medical distributors have an official function designated by the MHW. Officially, they act as an information channel which could have an adverse impact on patient care. But they also have the important function of reporting end-user prices to the MHW directly. MHW then sets reimbursement rates according to actual market prices.

- Until recently, manufacturers or importers told the distributors what price to charge end-users. Manufacturers and distributors could then effectively collude to set market prices at high rates. Now, however, the manufacturer is forbidden from setting end-user prices. Thus the distribution margin is determined by negotiations between the distributor and the end-user. The goal is to engineer a downward pricing spiral. In actuality, although there is downward pricing to some degree, the old system of collusion still operates, but below the surface.

- Distributors have two kinds of representatives. One is typically high-school educated and carries out the day-to-day grunt work, while the other typically has a university-level science degree and acts as a technical information provider, and at times, a troubleshooter.

- Traditionally, distributors purchased foreign products almost exclusively through a *shosha*. Tension has arisen because large distributors have sent their own representatives overseas in search of products. At any large American medical show, there are numerous Japanese representatives combing the floor for promising new products. Unfortunately, American companies have little ability to evaluate these companies.

8

John Meets the Great Doctor

The next morning Goro arranged a two-taxi caravan to transport them to meet Dr. Tani. The taxis pulled up in front of yet another nondescript gray building. They were led to a cramped office with exactly the same couch and two chairs and doilied coffee table that seems to occupy every office in Japan. Space was obviously at a premium and there were books and papers everywhere. After a fifteen-minute wait, the great doctor finally appeared.

Introductions were made, together with some rather stiff small talk. John looked at the *meishi*, or name card, that Dr. Tani had handed him. One side was Japanese; the other side was English, which read: Hiroyuki Tani, M.D., Ph.D., President, Japanese Association of Penile Implants. John was stunned. He didn't even know that such an association existed in Japan and here he was standing in front of its president.

Dr. Tani's manner was a bit stiff but friendly enough. What was perfectly clear to John was that every member of the entourage held Dr. Tani in awe. Even Takahashi spoke in polite tones with a bowed head with the doctor. John finally realized that he was sitting in front of The Man in penile implants in Japan.

As the formalities continued John had a chance to look around the office and reassess the situation. Every major book in the field seemed to be on the shelves, along with papers from every major conference of the last thirty years. He also noticed that Dr. Tani was lighting his fourth cigarette since their arrival. Finally, Dr. Tani broke through the small talk and addressed John in broken but discernible English, "Have you ever been to Pittsburgh?"

What a weird question, John thought as he nodded his head. John, who had in fact lived there for a year when he was a kid, knew it was one of the major centers of research in MTI's product area, and he had visited many times to talk with the R&D geeks about their research. That's all the great doctor needed. His eyes lit up. "I love Pittsburgh. I studied there in the early sixties, when I got my Ph.D. at the University of Pittsburgh. That is where I learned how to do penile implants. You know, I did the first penile implant in Japan in sixty-four."

Dr. Tani took another long drag on his cigarette and continued, "Since then I've become Japan's leading penile-implant surgeon." John was impressed and told him so. What a stroke of good luck to finally meet up with this man!

Goro was beginning to show signs of agitation at the shared experiences and growing camaraderie between Dr. Tani and John. He had originally told John that Dr. Tani had only five minutes to spare for them that morning. But Dr. Tani showed growing enthusiasm and no inclination whatsoever to conclude the meeting.

Dr. Tani began talking about MTI's products. He said he was very impressed with their cervical cancer detection sensor units. At this point the doctor and John dominated the conversation completely. They leaned towards each other over the now heaping full ashtray on the table as Dr. Tani talked about his current research in the laboratory and his latest advances. John tried to look impressed, but realized that MTI had done that stuff ten years ago.

John looked at Dr. Tani and decided to take a gamble and tell him about MTI's very latest breakthrough. The head office had sworn him to secrecy because the patents were still being filed worldwide, but John couldn't resist and figured there was little chance of Dr. Tani being able to duplicate the technology before MTI's product hit the market.

He leaned further across the table and whispered, "Do you want to know what our next model will do?" The Great Doctor almost quivered with excitement. "Oh, yes, yes." He looked like an eight-year old about to open his birthday present.

Glancing at the Morikawa guys and Takahashi who were desperately trying to pick up the thread of the conversation without being too obvious, John turned back to the Great Doctor and whispered with a fair amount of theatricality, "venereal disease detection sensors."

"No!" he gasped.

"Yes." John said, almost giggling with delight. "It will diagnose whether your partner has had any of a host of sexually transmitted diseases including AIDS, syphilis, gonorrhea, and chlamydia. And that's not all. It will also tell you if your partner has had intercourse within the past twenty-four hours."

Dr. Tani was practically bouncing up and down in his chair. "That's wonderful. *Sugoi!* Are you still using radio transmissions to transfer the data?"

John answered, "Yes. In fact, we are now developing a hand-held receiving unit..." They continued their conversation in undertones with the bystanders still trying to figure out what all the excitement was about. Finally, after a very considerable time the doctor indicated that he had to get back to work. But not before extending an invitation to dinner that evening to John, one that he immediately accepted to the chagrin of Goro.

One thing John did understand already about Japan was that a doctor may extend an invitation to dinner, but that did not mean that he was going to pay for it. John also understood that it was going to be a very expensive evening. One didn't take out the president of a major medical association and then feed him noodles and dumplings. He just hoped that Goro would get stuck with the bill, not MTI.

The great doctor was not a big eater. But he chain-smoked through dinner and consumed prodigious amounts of sake. The guy had to be in his seventies. John wondered how long someone could keep absorbing those amounts of alcohol and nicotine without suffering some kind of systemic collapse. At the end of dinner, Dr. Tani leaned over to Goro and mumbled something that made Goro sigh.

The entire group headed out the door and down the street. A couple of blocks later they stopped in front of a six-story building in the entertainment district, filled with bars and hostess clubs. Dr. Tani led the charge into the elevator and the troops followed. The doors opened and

they were greeted by an attractive mama-san in her forties who wel-
comed them and led them into a closet of a bar with chairs and tables
seemingly constructed by the munchkins from *The Wizard of Oz*. Dr.
Tani was already sucking on a fresh cigarette when a couple of very
young hostesses appeared on the scene, giggling and shouting Dr.
Tani's name with glee. He was obviously a regular and judging by the
beauty of the girls on either side of the Great Doctor, Goro was getting
stuck with a major league bill that night.

After much merriment and even more alcohol, Dr. Tani leaned over
the table to talk with John. Oddly enough, his English seemed to have
improved dramatically, or else John was simply losing his ear for the
ungrammatical. The great doctor's eyes were bloodshot, small globs of
spittle and partially masticated peanuts were randomly projected with
each consonant as he said in a low, serious tone, "Why are MTI's products so expensive in Japan?"

John glanced at Goro, who immediately picked up a glass of something and proposed a loud toast to the young beauty who had been rubbing the inside of his thigh most of the evening. John played it cool and
merely shrugged his shoulders.

The doctor continued. "Why doesn't MTI do any clinical research in
Japan?"

With that question, John could not hold back his amazement. "What
do you mean, no clinical research in Japan? We do lots of clinical
research. Morikawa spends a considerable amount of money every year
on clinical research." John recalled that Morikawa claimed to spend significant amounts on research every year. Now he wasn't so sure.

"I don't think so," Dr. Tani responded with more than a touch of
indignation. "As president of the association, I would surely know if
any research was being sponsored in the field of penile implants.
Nothing, absolutely nothing happens in this field without my partici-
pation. To get your products approved for sale in Japan you must go
through the *gakkai* and to use the *gakkai*, you must go through me."

John's composure started to slip a bit. He stared at Goro while he
replied to Dr. Tani, "I had no idea. Forgive me for my ignorance."

Dr. Tani continued, warming up to the task of educating the foreigner. "There is also the issue of reimbursement. You know, we can

hardly use your products because they are not listed on the reimbursement schedule by the MHW. You know reimbursement, don't you. It's called *hoken tensu* here in Japan. Because they are not reimbursed, only the wealthiest of patients can use the products. What a shame! So many more could benefit if MTI would only did what it should do in Japan."

John pulled his eyes from Dr. Tani and aimed his glance at Goro, who refused to make eye contact. The bottom of his glass was apparently fascinating. John realized that his knuckles had turned white from gripping the sides of the little table. It was very quiet, and homicide was not an option. Even their cute companions, Yuki-chan and Tomo-chan, seemed to realize that the harmony of the universe was in jeopardy. Finally, Dr. Tani stood up and said, "*Ah, soro-soro jikan.* It's time to go." Goro was off the hook this time, but John knew that a moment of truth was rapidly approaching. He was to leave for Los Angeles the next day and give his report to the head office on the situation in Japan. Big Ed was waiting.

John's Lessons

- In Japan there are associations for virtually everything. The term for association in Japanese is *gakkai*. Basically, these associations are horizontal groups bringing together people with the same interest or affiliation. They have no official governmental function and they are not regulated, but they do wield tremendous power. The various Japanese ministries go to these associations for guidance on the approval of products and ultimately for the initial reimbursement decision.

- All medical products in Japan require *shonin*, or regulatory approval. For new products, Japanese clinical trials are required in most cases. The traditional manner of doing clinical trials was to go to the related association and entice the president or other high-ranking association official to become your honorary chairman. He would then assign association members to be the primary research investigators.

- The association president and leaders are usually chosen more for their political clout than for their technical expertise. Rising to the top of any association is a vicious dog-eat-dog process requiring keen political ambition and access to persons of influence or power. The traditional edge is to have the past association head anoint one as his successor. Other advantages include links with foreign universities, English skills, or status as a ground-breaking researcher.

- The *gakkai* system has the merit of providing information and control. However, the *gakkai* system has fallen into some disrepute as of late. The HIV-contaminated blood scandal, in which at least 1,800 hemophiliacs were infected with HIV as a result of using unheated blood products is a major factor. It is alleged that an association president delayed approval of heated products in order to protect the market position of Japanese companies. The *gakkai* system can also can retard innovation since all power rests with older leaders whose knowledge is dated.

- The irony of the "power broker" *gakkai* system is that it can undermine consensus, which is normally the rule in Japanese institutions. This is in direct contrast to the FDA in the United States, which requires open advisory panels that sink into endless discussions and then vote to recommend approval or not. Recent discussions in Japan have touched on the possibility of adopting the FDA style of advisory panels in order to limit the control of the power brokers of the *gakkai*.

9

John Learns about Shonin Power

John arrived around 10:30 a.m. at LAX on the United flight from Narita. He felt OK. He had learned that when going west across the Pacific it was a good idea to catch a few Zs on the plane and hit the ground running in L.A. He grabbed one of the Hertz shuttle buses, jumped into a Lincoln Town Car (hey, it's L.A.) and cruised toward the MTI headquarters in Santa Monica.

Halfway there he realized just how long he had been out of the States and how completely he had shifted gears in order to exist in Japan. He was struck by how big Americans were. "Man, has everyone gained fifty pounds, or what? And, there are just so many foreigners." With a twinge, John realized how stupid that sounded. Here, he was the native. Japanese were the foreigners, or *gaijin*.

The drive, though, was pure pleasure. After the mute misery of a Tokyo summer followed by the even worse fall typhoon season, John was overwhelmed by the casual beauty of a normal Santa Monica day. Seventy degrees, nice ocean breeze. Not bad, he thought. He pulled into the MTI parking lot at the corner of Twenty-sixth and Colorado.

MTI's headquarters was a soaring erection of glass and chrome, overtly phallic in its surge skyward. It wasn't exactly the Crystal Cathedral, but no one would have let words like elegant or tasteful collide in the same sentence as MTI. Formed in the early seventies by Dr. John Knowland, MTI was the physical expression of Knowland's unbounded ego and talent. Knowland was L.A.'s most famous (or notorious) cosmetic surgeon, and parlayed a telegenic presence on local TV together with an indefatigable ability to liposuction fat, trim tummies, and pump up penises. Knowland's fate as a wealthy, slim, and silver-haired Beverly Hills surgeon was changed dramatically one day when one of his patients, while under anesthesia, muttered something about radio-controlled penile implants. The rest was history. Knowland stole the idea, shafted his partner, started MTI, and then took it public in the IPO boom of 1984.

John marveled at American entrepreneurship. Today, Dr. Knowland was "retired," with stock options approaching $500 million and his own television talk show on KTLA in L.A. He was the lead-in for Oprah. It doesn't get any better than that.

Dr. Knowland was gone from the day-to-day management of MTI. But his vision remained (as well as the monstrosity of a headquarters), ably served by the president and CEO of MTI, Big Ed Polick. John knew Big Ed, but he wasn't sure if Big Ed knew him. Befitting his name, Big Ed was six-foot-six and the kind of man who did not reflect long before making a decision. Every sentence contained at least one expletive or threat. On the management spectrum, Big Ed was about as far away from the infamous Japanese management style as humanly possible. Big Ed gave orders to the troops to charge the barbed wire and then shot anyone who didn't move. Yes, Big Ed was the BSD of MTI.

John was not looking forward to his presentation on the Japan situation. John knew that the information prepared for the report by JBBD would elicit, first, disbelief and second, if believed, blind rage. He knew MTI's "corporate culture" well enough to know that merely being the messenger of such bad news, if not actually enough to get one shot, was enough to derail a corporate career. But John also knew that he was close to that invisible time line that would make him "responsible" for everything that ever happened in Japan. If he didn't do something soon to change MTI's direction in Japan he was going to be lying face down in the dirt, arrows in his back, his family stolen by hostiles and his cabin on fire.

John decided to give Big Ed both barrels right between the eyes. Within twenty minutes of lights-out at the presentation, Big Ed was pacing the length of the conference room cursing Morikawa, Japan, and just about anything else west of the Pacific Coast Highway. He was incensed. "Those rotten, lying bastards. How could they do this to us?"

John's presentation was a shambles. He tried to preserve a measure of calm and provide some background on why this had happened in Japan. But no one was listening. Everyone at the conference table was vying for Big Ed's attention, nodding their heads, and muttering imprecations about the treacherous Japanese and evil Morikawa. He thought he even heard someone mention Pearl Harbor. Big Ed was completely worked up now. He looked at John, pointed his finger and said, "Get rid of the sonsabitches. No argument. Just do it." With that, he summoned whatever dignity was left and strode from the conference room. That basically concluded the presentation.

It was not exactly a coherent Japan strategy, John thought. But it did have the benefit of simplicity. Within seconds, John was alone with his immediate boss, Chuck Warren. Chuck was the ultimate corporate survivor. A back-slapper and sports-page reader, he was always on the right side of the corporate fence, no matter how many times the wind changed. "I told you Big Ed would be pissed. He set up that relationship and he loved the Morikawa boys. Rumor has it that Morikawa himself was getting Big Ed laid every trip to Japan."

John was miffed. "They never offered to get me laid," he thought while Chuck droned on about the meeting. "It's a good thing you had that report done. Big Ed never would have believed you without the back-up. You woulda been humpin' NeoProbes in Bulgaria without it. That was a stroke of genius." Chuck slapped his back and said, "Hey, did you see the Lakers-Sonics game?"

It was a very short trip stateside. Like it or not, Big Ed had given him his marching orders and there was nothing else to do at MTI. By 11:00 a.m. the next day John was winging his way back to Japan. This time all he could think about was Hitomi. Sweet, shy, lovable, bubbly, giggling Hitomi. His heart was in the clouds. He was in love. This was the real thing. His plane touched down at Narita at 6:37 p.m. and by 9:10 he was at the Passion Fruit Club in Shibuya. That was where his Hitomi was gainfully employed and, sometime that night, John asked her to marry him.

The next morning, his back sore from a combination of the long flight and the irrepressible bedroom gymnastics of the passionate Hitomi, John felt no pain. In fact, he felt great. Today was the day when he would follow Big Ed's instructions and tell Morikawa to take a hike. OTC would be in full motion in a few hours.

John took a taxi to work which happened to go down Sakurada-street near Shibakoen. On a moment's impulse, John asked the taxi driver to stop at the JBBD office near the Tokyo Tower. He took the elevator and asked the receptionist if Bruce was available by any chance. He was and she told him to feel free to head down the hallway to his office. As usual, John found him typing like a fiend and listening to the Doors.

"Bruce, you can congratulate us." John said, as the final chords of "L.A. Woman" died down on the speakers. "I just wanted to stop by and tell you that your report was a big hit at MTI's executive meeting."

Bruce barely looked up from the screen, "That's nice."

"Also, I thought you might be interested to hear that Big Ed gave me the go-ahead to fire Morikawa and break the contract with them. The deed will be done in less than an hour. Operation Take Control will be a success."

"What?" Bruce barked, finally jerking his gaze away from the computer monitor.

"We're going to fire the bastards," John said, still beaming.

"Well, if you do, you're screwed." Bruce replied. John's face lost some of its post-whatever glow. Bruce jumped to his feet and pointed to the conference room. "Let's talk. And this is billable time."

John started to protest, but a little voice in his head whispered words to the effect of shut up and listen. He followed Bruce into the room and sat down. Bruce was already sketching out a mind map on the white board. "Who owns the *shonin*, you know, the regulatory approvals for MTI's products in Japan." he asked John.

"Morikawa does, of course. You know that." John was losing his bounce a bit.

"Given that situation, you are at least a year away from selling your first post-Morikawa product in Japan. That's how long it will take you to get the *shonin* in MTI's name and get reimbursement for the products. As I recall, your contract with Morikawa is an exclusive for all of Japan and it still has three years to run. It even has a provision for an automatic rollover if they achieve a five percent annual growth rate. Right?"

"That's right.," responded John. "But the contract also contains clauses that allow for its cancellation in the event of bad faith or dishonesty. It is the position of our Board of Directors and legal counsel that Morikawa has acted in bad faith and with dishonesty, thereby breaching the contract." John was proud of his legalese, but his words lacked confidence on this side of the Pacific. Maybe the image of Sakota's nose-blowing antics popped into his consciousness at that moment.

Bruce pushed on. "Well, what about their distributors? Do you even know who they are? What about your customers? Who are they and how are you going to service them ninety minutes from now when you gun down Morikawa at high noon on the streets of Tokyo?"

John cringed in his chair. He knew what Bruce said was true, but he also sensed that he could handle most of the problems with time and lots of work. The one thing, though, that he could simply not work around was the fact that Morikawa owned the *shonin* for MTI's products. That was the gun to their head. John was mulling this over when Bruce suddenly went quiet, his shoulders slumped and his arms fell to his sides. "Do what you want. It's your business. I've seen this a thousand times, but I can't do it for you. But, remember one thing, John. Japan is a very unforgiving place. People have very long memories and you don't get a second chance if you screw up. Think about it."

John left the JBBD office feeling very subdued. Basically, he was caught between a rock and a hard place. Big Ed's instructions had been pretty specific: Fire the bastards immediately. But everything that Bruce said was true. John felt that with time he could learn to handle the specifics of the Japan market. But the *shonin* were the golden keys—without them he wouldn't get a chance to ante up and play the game. He knew that two years with zero sales meant he could kiss his career goodbye at MTI.

Goro met him in the lobby of the Morikawa building. He smiled tentatively, obviously expecting the worst after the meeting with Dr. Tani and John's trip back to L.A. to visit MTI. John took a deep breath and cast his fate to the winds. He smiled back, slapped Goro on the back and said, "Hey, did you see the Grand Sumo tournament yesterday? How about that Takanohana guy?"

John's Lessons

- The *shonin* is the "golden key" to the Japanese market. For all intents and purposes, the *shonin*-holder is the market owner in Japan. If your Japanese partner holds the *shonin*, then, for all practical purposes, any favorable clauses which allow you to cancel the contract are void. Ending the relationship would entail either paying incredible fees to pass the *shonin* to you or to your designee. Or it would mean starting over, possibly with clinical trials. Your products would be out of the market for years.

- In negotiations, Japanese typically position the regulatory approval as being a burden on their side, which it certainly is. The foreign technology holder invariably allows the importer or distributor hold the *shonin*.

- There are methods of having a foreign-owned company hold its own *shonin*. Not only does this offer the foreign entity a strong bargaining chip during initial negotiations, it also offers long-term flexibility.

- A *shonin* is an approval by the MHW to either manufacturer or import a medical product. It must be applied for in combination with a *kyoka* which is similar to an import permit. One entity, for reasons of clarity, may hold a *shonin* and from that one or more different entities may hold the *kyoka*, referenced to a single *shonin*.

- Holding a *kyoka* for import of medical products requires that an entity have been granted a Class I, II, or III medical import license. Among other requirements, the importer must have adequate and suitable warehouse space, a pharmacist, physician, or dentist on staff and it must have a separate room, suitably equipped for quality control. In reality, many small importers never or rarely use their quality control room or equipment and the pharmacist is a friend who agrees to lend his or her name and license to the application.

- An importer will almost always satisfy the requirements to hold a *shonin*. However, if you wish to designate a trusted party to hold a *shonin*, it is possible under the in-country caretaker section of the Japanese Pharmaceutical Affairs Law. An in-country caretaker must have adequate educational and professional experience based on the technology for which he would be responsible. Preferably he or she would have a doctoral degree, but this is not mandatory. For acceptance as an in-country caretaker a company needs a complete resumé, educational transcripts, and a copy of the executed in-country caretaker contract must be attached with the *shonin* application.

- An in-country caretaker has several important roles: 1) meeting in-house documentation requirements; 2) managing a notification system whereby he can inform the manufacturer within fifteen days of any initial reports of products which could adversely effect patient care; and 3) ensuring that any reports of adverse patient results outside of Japan are reported to all users within fifteen days of the report. The last two points are typically done through agreements with distributors.

- Below are several ways a foreign company can structure an agreement to protect its long-term regulatory control and grab the "golden key:"

1) Hold the *shonin* through an in-country caretaker and allow the distributor(s) to hold the *kyoka* and independently import the products. If anything happens, the company can cut off the distributor at will and appoint one or more others.

2) If the distributor is uncomfortable with this arrangement, it is possible to set up a parallel *shonin* system. If the foreign technology holder should decide to move on he may simply refuse to supply the product. The distributor's *shonin* essentially becomes ineffective.

3) The foreign technology holder can contractually provide for the distributor to pass the *shonin* to the importer the in the event of default. This is only recommended in cases where you are dealing with a large Japanese company with a significant presence in the

West. Suing in Japan would be a long, cumbersome, and probably useless exercise.

10

John Resurrects OTC

John could tell that Big Ed was really pissed off when he picked up the phone at his apartment at 3:20 a.m. Maybe it was the string of loud profanities. It was a good thing that Hitomi didn't stir when John took Big Ed's opening salvo; in fact, Hitomi wasn't stirring for much of anything these days, John thought as Big Ed blasted him again.

"What can be so difficult about firing these sonsabitches? If you haven't got the balls, I bet I can find someone here that'll do it."

Obviously, Big Ed had gotten John's fax detailing the issues involved in "firing the sonsabitches" as Big Ed put it so succinctly. John had spent considerable time analyzing the issues and providing a detailed response to each one. He also quickly realized that Big Ed had read half of page one of the twelve-page fax before picking up the phone and dropping a dime. Hitomi began snoring as John gently responded to Big Ed's diatribe, "Ed, no matter what, we can't forget that Morikawa owns the regulatory approvals for our products."

"Well, buy new ones," Big Ed shouted into the phone.

"That's exactly what we're planning to do, but it will take two years. In the meantime, we could lose all of our Japan sales if Morikawa pulled the rug out from us. We would have to start from scratch."

"Sonsabitches," Big Ed repeated and hung up.

John realized that he had been given a reprieve of sorts. Big Ed's anger was focused solely on Morikawa, but it wouldn't take long before he looked for other targets and the collateral damage would be awesome. Wide awake, John nervously planned his next step. He rolled next to Hitomi, hoping that a little slap and tickle might take his mind off his problems. Hitomi only added to them when she muttered, "Sam, not now."

John wondered whether it wouldn't be a good idea for him to become a guinea pig and get an MTI implant of his own. At least then he might be able to confirm or disprove his growing suspicions about Hitomi's nocturnal activities. At 5:00 a.m. John finally fell asleep.

First thing the next morning John had Miss Bamba get Bruce on the line. "Bruce, do you have time for lunch today?"

"Sure, but if you want to talk business, I'm going to hit the clock."

Mercenary, John thought. "OK, then I'm picking the spot. And be prepared for an earful."

It didn't take long for Bruce to adopt his lecturing tone of voice once he heard the situation from John. "First of all, Morikawa is not the evil empire. Someone from MTI, Big Ed probably, came to Japan years ago. They didn't do any research or act with due diligence and signed a contract with the first Japanese they saw with a bit of distinguished gray hair and some money in his pocket. Morikawa simply did what any aggressive company would do and took full advantage of the opportunities handed to them by MTI. There was nothing unethical about it. MTI deserves what it got."

"Yeah, sure, but look at it from our point of view for a second. They have marked up our products so high that only a few people can afford them, they failed to get reimbursement and they have let our competitors, Japanese companies with inferior products, grab the lion's share of the market. They had a moral obligation to protect our interests. At the very least they should have told us what was happening. We acted in good faith with them and they acted in bad faith!" John was getting pretty worked up when Bruce interrupted.

"Give me a break! You're big boys. You should have known what was going on. Think about it, John. As a businessman, what would you rather do? Sell 100 units a year at $10,000 each or 1,000 units at $1,000 each? The revenue is the same in either case. But with low volume, high margin sales you do not need an expensive service or sales infrastructure. Your profits will be several orders of magnitude higher. Market share and other strategic factors are the responsibility of the technology holder, not the distributor. To walk away and think that a distributor will act in your best interests is simply naive." Bruce had turned red and his voice was loud enough that people at nearby tables were beginning to stare.

"OK, OK," John said, holding up his hand. "The fact is we're just spinning our wheels here. The past is past. What I need are solutions for the future. And I need them fast. What do you think I should do?"

Bruce thought for a few moments and finally replied, "Assuming that you have really decided to dump Morikawa, which I believe is your best long-term strategy, you have several options. First, you can hire your own regulatory staff and plow through the approval process and then apply for your own *shonin*. Second, you can work with an outside service and contract out the *shonin* process. Third, you can go to Morikawa and negotiate to have the *shonin* transferred directly to MTI or another qualified party."

"Having Morikawa transfer the *shonin* to us seems like the best and fastest way to get going here." John said, as much to himself as to Bruce. "How much do you think we would have to pay them?"

"Well, judging from past experience, I would say you are looking at fifty-thousand dollars apiece for approvals for the kind of products that MTI sells. Of course, that does not include any clinical trial costs."

"That's great," John responded with a touch of hope in his voice. "That means that we would only have to pay Morikawa three-hundred thousand dollars for the six *shonin* that they hold on MTI's products."

"Whoa, pardner," Bruce said. "That's three-hundred thousand just to complete the regulatory approval process on your own. The fact is that the value of the *shonin* is much greater for Morikawa. All it takes is some simple math to calculate the value." For a moment, John was horrified that Bruce might actually start writing on the linen tablecloth, but Bruce ripped out a piece of paper from his notebook and began scribbling.

Cost of goods/yr:	$3 million
Margin add-on:	$6 million

Cost of business:	$2 million
Profit per year:	$4 million
2 years:	$8 million

"You're not going to like these numbers, but here they are. If MTI does its own approvals and cuts out Morikawa, it will take about eight million U.S. out of Morikawa's pocket over the next two years. I suppose if you negotiated well, you could get the *shonin* back for maybe half that amount."

John whistled. "Wow, that's a lot of money. There's no way we could pay that. If I went to Big Ed and asked him for four million to negotiate our way out of the Morikawa contract he would feed me alive to his pet piranhas and put it on videotape as part of a training exercise for new employees. Now I see that the *shonin* really are the golden key to the market here."

"If option three is a no go, I suggest that you look into either hiring a regulatory staff or out-sourcing the project," Bruce quietly suggested.

Hiring a regulatory staff seemed like a pretty unlikely funding request to John also. "I guess that means I need to look for someone to do this for us. Know anyone?"

"As a matter of fact, I do. I'll introduce you to JBBD's director of regulatory affairs, Dr. Morita. But I suggest that you talk to a couple of companies in order to get a feel for what's out there."

Dr. Morita had an athletic look to him. He was lean and tall, with only slight tufts of gray at his temples. His English was pretty good. In a slow, deliberate manner he walked John through the entire MHW regulatory process. "We need complete copies of your FDA 510(k) materials. Once we have these, we will determine what needs to be translated and what other materials need to generated. Your generic implants probably will not require any clinical trials. But your new products, the implants with the sensor tips, will almost certainly need to have local clinical trials designed to demonstrate both safety and efficacy." John nodded, but looked sleepy.

"Man, I hate regulatory work. It's a refined torture, death by boredom," John thought. He replied to Dr. Morita, "Morikawa doesn't have *shonin* for those products either, so we'll have to start from scratch in any case." He paused for a second, then asked a question he knew was sure to produce heartburn. "How much will the clinical trials cost?"

"Bruce, have you explained to John-san about the difference between *tatemae* and *honne*?" Dr. Morita asked.

Bruce nodded, "He's beginning to understand a bit." Bruce seemed even more bored by the regulatory stuff than John.

"Well, John, the new MHW (Koseisho) regulations stipulate that MTI will have to pay for all the treatments surrounding the procedure being performed for the clinical trial. As you can guess, this can be very expensive. My estimate is that it could cost fifteen thousand dollars per patient for the medicine, hospitalization, surgery, and other associated costs. Koseisho requires a minimum of two trial sites with a minimum of thirty patients each. Roughly speaking, the cost for the clinical trial would be around one million dollars."

John looked like he was going to hyperventilate. "Are you telling me that Morikawa paid that much for their clinical trials?"

Both Bruce and Dr. Morita burst out laughing. John felt a touch annoyed, but waited until Bruce replied. "Only rich foreign companies pay that much money. Usually, they pay it to unscrupulous in-country caretakers who take the money and then never pay it to the hospitals. That's the *honne*. Even if a company paid the full amount directly to the clinical site, the hospital would turn around and invariably charge the insurance agency anyway, thus getting a double pop on the procedures."

John looked confused. Dr. Morita continued. "It means that you have to negotiate with the hospital and the investigator directly on a case-by-case basis. The bottom line is that each of the patients in the trial was going in for treatment and surgery anyway. Thus entering the trial is subsequent to the decision to enroll the patient in the trial. It's kind of supply and demand. If the investigator is really interested in the product and believes that he can get some good publications out of the trial, he will be willing to negotiate. MTI's in a good spot here. Because your products are cutting edge, we can assume that leading doctors will want to participate in the clinical trial. That means we can work around those fees."

John looked like he was catching on. "OK, so what is it going to cost MTI to run a typical trial?"

Dr. Morita continued. "There are two charges that we will have trouble avoiding. One is the appreciation money paid directly to the hospital. This is a semi-official charge, but the amount is negotiable and then paid to the university hospital conducting the clinical trial. The money then filters down to the various departments. It's hard to calculate exactly right now, but you can expect to pay between two and three thousand U.S. per patient enrolled. Since your product will require 60 cases, we can figure around $180,000 at the top end. Also, post approval MTI will be required to monitor ten percent of the clinical trial cases as part of the PMS, or post-marketing survey. Let's figure two-hundred thousand dollars for the appreciation money."

John had a sneaking suspicion that Dr. Morita was not finished.

"Then, of course, there are the clinical management fees. JBBD usually covers these fees on a monthly retainer basis, depending on how many patients are enrolled and where and how many investigators and sites there are. Lastly, we make the manufacturer pay for all entertainment expenses for the doctors." Dr. Morita stopped to think for a moment, then continued. "By the way, who is the president of the Penile Implant Gakkai?"

"Dr. Tani from Nagano," Bruce blurted out.

"That's a tough break," said Dr. Morita. "We will need to increase the entertainment budget."

John's Lessons

- In many cases, foreign companies fail to do their homework in Japan. They seldom investigate the market or their prospective partners. Then they blame the "closed" Japanese market for results for which they have only themselves to blame.

- Foreign companies must keep a sharp eye out for the "low volume, high price" strategy often adopted by Japanese companies selling foreign technologies. It makes perfect bottom-line sense for the

Japanese distributor. As a result, it is the responsibility of the foreign technology holder to support market share and other strategic business policies.

- Until April 1996, manufacturers doing clinical trials in Japan needed to pay "appreciation money," and provide products at no cost to the trial. But, as of 1997, Koseisho has ruled that a company must also pay for certain therapies surrounding patient support. Koseisho's argument is simply one of economics. Industry has countered by claiming that the patients would have inevitably required treatment anyway and industry should only be forced to pay the direct costs incurred as a result of the clinical trial.

- The *honne* of the situation appears to be that the company doesnot pay for the surrounding care (although there are usually foreign companies that don't know any better). Hospitals have also been known to apply for reimbursement, essentially double-dipping.

- In most cases, the reality is dictated by the power brokers of the *gakkai*. They are essentially above the law. There is also a certain amount of negotiation possible with Koseisho, which tends to be understanding if the investigator and manufacturer approaches with a fair plan fulfilling all of the *tatemae* obligations.

- The system of "appreciation money" is a difficult practice to pin down. It stems from the days, not so long ago, when clinical trials had the whiff of graft about them. In the old days, clinical trials were very convenient. A company simply decided on what outcome it wished, paid an appropriate amount to the doctor and it got the results. Koseisho was typically only interested in safety and gave local manufacturers a lot of room in terms of efficacy claims. This "look the other way" policy resulted in products such as magnets that are pasted on the back for arthritis and other ailments. It also led to some widely used drugs, such as multibillion-dollar coenzyme Q10 derivatives for stroke indications, which have very poor efficacy but are unquestionably safe. The growing issue is that these products are reimbursable, and are a financial burden on the health insurance system.

11

Six Months Later...

"But, Hitomi!" John half pleaded and half screamed, as she hurled another of John's old wrestling trophies across the room at him. He barely deflected it with his already bleeding forearm. So much for the shy, sweet, bubbly and giggling Hitomi. Thwack! "No, not my college beer glass," John pleaded. Crash. John bolted for the door and slammed it behind him. It was time to get out of Dodge.

John had been married for six months. The first week was pretty good, but it was downhill from there. The first inkling of trouble came when Hitomi suddenly announced that from now on she would handle all of the money matters for the household. Her first official act as the Minister of Household Finance was to establish a monthly allowance for John. John howled in protest, but she curtly dismissed him and said it was the Japanese custom. He couldn't believe it at first, but had it confirmed by all of his Japanese friends who commiserated with John and shared stories of how they got by late in the month before payday. Worst of all, Hitomi wouldn't even tell him how much money they had. "Shut up and mind your own business," was sweet Hitomi's stock response to any question on money matters.

Sitting on the curb near his apartment, dazed and bleeding, John wondered how this myth of the sweet, subservient Japanese woman had been disseminated throughout the West. But relief was in sight. Just down the street John saw one of Japan's great contributions to modern civilization, a beer vending machine. "Damn," he thought as he checked his wallet. Only three-thousand yen and no credit cards—Hitomi had confiscated all of them. Still, it was enough to buy a couple of cans and plot his next steps.

John returned to his little perch and alternated between drinking his half-liter can of Kirin and rubbing it across his forearms, which had been deeply gouged by Hitomi's fingernails. He actually managed a laugh as he recalled her utter horror at breaking one of her nails during the attack. He wasn't even sure why she was mad. It wasn't a language barrier.

It was like she was two completely different people. There was Hitomi the girlfriend, who was sweet, shy and fun-loving. Now there was Hitomi the wife, who was all business and fond of quoting the Japanese adage that the perfect husband was *jobu de rusu*, or healthy and gone. The Passion Fruit Club Hitomi had been vaporized. The worst thing was that she had started rationing sex. She used it almost like a reward system. John felt like one of Pavlov's dogs being paper trained. If she asked him to do the dishes, he got an erection. Doing the laundry was near orgasmic bliss.

Compared to his deteriorating domestic situation, John's business situation was even worse. Much worse. The past six months had seen a steady slide downhill as a result of a few really bad decisions. John took another hit on his can of beer as he reviewed his tale of woe.

JBBD had given John a detailed proposal for their services as in-country caretaker and manager of the proposed clinical trials. The numbers were right in line with those they had given him during the meeting at the JBBD office. But he took Bruce's advice and got two additional quotes on the project. One of the quotes came from Biomedical Industries Incorporated, or BII, and it was less than half of the JBBD quote. John couldn't resist the bargain and employed them. It was a major league mistake. Bruce had warned him that some companies practice the "stone soup" strategy with small foreign companies needing regulatory services. That is, they start off with a very small amount of money to get the business rolling, then they keep adding fee after fee once the foreign client is in too deep to pull out. "Soup from a stone, imagine that!" John thought bitterly.

Well, BII had nailed him good. John could just imagine Mr. Kawasaki, the president of BII, dining on MTI's tab. Just this morning one of Kawasaki's ever-changing cast of henchmen called up John and requested that MTI pay two thousand U.S. for revenue stamps. After that call, John went back and reviewed the proposals and realized that he was already twenty percent over the budget quoted by JBBD and he had a sneaking suspicion that Kawasaki had more unpleasant surprises in store for him. Luckily, John thought, he had taken Bruce's advice on one thing, though. In his contract with BII he had added a clause that allowed MTI to change to another in-country caretaker at any time and that BII was required to transfer all files and materials upon demand.

John and Bruce still saw each other from time to time in an official capacity at the ACCJ medical sub-committee meetings and they got together once a month to play poker as part of small group of seven or eight foreigners, all presidents of medical companies in Japan. Poker was the ostensible reasonable for the get-togethers, but it also served as a valuable release valve for the guys. They played cards, drank excessively, and swapped war stories about doing business in Japan. Everyone had a great time. One thing John had noticed during the games was that Bruce didn't seem to hold a grudge about John's decision to go with BII. In fact, it was Bruce who got John invited into the group.

Maybe it was too much Scotch; maybe it was losing a couple hundred bucks on some god-awful poker hands; or maybe it was the combined strain of a collapsing marriage and a business in the toilet that broke John one night after a game. It didn't start that way. The game finished up about 1:00 a.m., the way it usually did, with the guys staggering out to find taxis to get home and probably furious wives. John would have appreciated even an angry wife at that point. But with nowhere to go and no one to be with, John pulled Bruce aside and asked him if he would be willing to knock back one more before heading home. Bruce hesitated, but relented after taking a careful look at John.

They popped into a stand-up shot bar near the Roi Building in Roppongi called The Wonder Bar and ordered a round. John had barely managed a sip of his Scotch before he started shaking all over.

"Hey, man what's wrong? Are you OK," Bruce asked as he grabbed John's arm to steady him. "You're in tough shape. Hitomi again?"

John seemed to recover a bit and took another sip. "That's only half of it. But let's just say it hasn't been an idyllic marriage. I haven't told anyone, and please keep this a secret, but I've been staying in capsule hotels the past few weeks."

Bruce stared at him, blinking once. "Jeez, man, what happened?"

That's all John needed and the whole story poured out. "Hitomi kicked me out of the apartment a while back and I just didn't know what to do. She beat me. Threw stuff at me and, now, won't even let me back in the place. That's bad, but it gets crazier. Last night I stopped by the apartment to get some of my stuff and found two Jamaican dudes, running around nude and stoned out of their brains on pot. It was ugly."

Bruce just stared now, transfixed by John's story. "That's pretty bad, all right. But it's kind of funny, too."

John glanced balefully at Bruce, "Yeah, right, real funny." He drained his glass and signaled for one more, but Bruce stayed pat. "The real funny thing is that my business situation may be worse than my marriage, or whatever is left of it."

"Do you remember those BII guys, the in-country caretakers?"

"Yeah, how could I forget? I've been hearing stories about BII at our poker games for years."

"Well, I'll spare you the worst details, but they did exactly what you said they would do. It's been seven months now and they're more than twenty-percent over the quotation that you folks gave me. And the ante keeps going up! I just don't know what to do."

Self-pity oozed from John's voice, something that Bruce found very irritating. "That's a real shame about Hitomi. No one should have to open the door in his own place to that kind of thing. But this stuff about BII is complete bullshit. You're a businessman and you were warned. Deal with it!"

"Well, it's not that simple. Let me finish. Somehow or another, Morikawa found out about us going after parallel *shonin* for our products. I know that I didn't tell anyone. And I know that you wouldn't tell anyone. That leaves BII as the culprit. That Kawasaki-san is a real piece of work."

"Tokyo's a small place," Bruce interjected. "There are no secrets here for long."

"Now everyone at Morikawa is pissed off and calling me dishonest. Can you believe it, Morikawa calling me dishonest? Morikawa himself wrote a letter to Big Ed telling him that the only solution to the problem of my despicable behavior was to lower prices. What a bastard!"

"That's too bad, John. But you knew this was going to be tough."

"Thanks for the sympathy, Bruce. Yeah, I knew it would be tough, but I didn't think I'd wake up in the slime every morning."

With a sigh and some reluctance, Bruce asked "Is there more?"

John took a deep breath and a big gulp, "Yeah, there's more."

It was very, very late when John stumbled into the Kanda Capsule Hotel, a few blocks from the Marunouchi exit of Tokyo Station. Home, sweet home. The night clerk was delighted, as always, to see John. "Too much drink," he laughed. "Too much drink," John giggled. "I think I'll take a bath."

John slipped into the steaming hot water of the bath, made the obligatory "ahh" sound, and only then took stock of his bath mates. Two were inebriated businessmen like John and two were *chinpira*, or lower-ranked mobsters. The *chinpira* were clearly second-tier, something unmistakable about the poorly done tattoos on their chests, arms and butts. After his quick survey, John closed his eyes and ignored them. He reviewed the evening and marveled. A plan was beginning to form and he could feel the onset of a dead cat bounce, the upward bounce after hitting rock bottom. He made a mental list to do the following:

1. Hire a private detective to get pictures of Hitomi and her most recent bedmate(s). File for divorce. Change bank ac-counts. Cancel credit cards.

2. Give his landlord the required sixty days notice. He was getting ripped off anyway.

3. Tell Kawasaki at BII to transfer all of the *shonin* materials to Dr. Morita at JBBD.

4. Sit down with Morikawa and tell them that MTI was getting its own *shonin* for the purpose of expanding distribution in Japan. It's MTI's technology and only right to do whatever it takes to build the business in Japan.

It wasn't exactly a double-blind study, but John had discovered that the intensity of hangovers seemed to decrease with practice. Maybe fewer brain cells meant less pain. John could feel the dead cat bounce already as he embarked on his quest for redemption.

Miss Bamba, adroitly, had located the best private detective company in Tokyo and John learned that it was only a matter of money. Imagine that! The detective said that with some good shots of Hitomi doing naked acrobatics with the stoned Jamaican duo, he should come out OK in divorce court.

The real estate guy seemed more than happy to hear John's request. Apparently, the neighbors had been complaining. There was the shouting, object hurling and slamming doors awhile back, only to be replaced recently by grunting and rhythmic banging at all hours of the night.

The meeting with Kawasaki of BII was not so pleasant. It began with gurgling noises. As soon as John mentioned MTI's desire to replace BII as their in-country caretaker in Japan, Kawasaki began making odd, sucking noises. They grew in intensity when John asked Kawasaki to transfer all of MTI's files immediately to Dr. Morita at JBBD. At the mere mention of Dr. Morita and JBBD, Kawasaki's nostrils flared and he said, "That is quite impossible. Our company policy is that regulatory files never leave the office."

At this point, John pulled out their contract and read the clause noting that BII was obligated to transfer all regulatory files immediately upon request to the designated party.

"There must be some mistake," Kawasaki replied. "As your in-country caretaker we are required by the Koseisho to keep all documentation in our possession. That is the law."

"First of all, Kawasaki-san, as of today, you are no longer the in-country caretaker for MTI. Second, since you have not yet secured a *shonin* for any of our products, there is no *shonin* for you to protect. Third, you are contractually obligated to transfer those files. Are you getting the picture?"

"John-san, my good friend. Please calm yourself. We are only here to help you. You are a foreigner here. You cannot be expected to understand the many complexities and contradictions of Japanese culture and society. . . ."

John sat and listened for half an hour to Kawasaki's version of the "Japan-is-too-difficult-for-you-foreigners-to-understand" speech. Finally, he walked out, empty-handed. BII would not relinquish the files. The next stop was Morikawa.

John's Lessons

- There are a large number of in-country caretakers in Japan. In some cases, they are retired regulatory executives or even current regulatory employees of pharmaceutical companies. It has almost become a cottage industry. Other in-country caretakers include consulting companies and Clinical Research Organizationz (CROs). There have been a considerable number of stories about foreign companies getting duped by their in-country caretaker. It is typically very difficult to change in mid-stream, providing an incentive to add on costs once the company is hooked.

- There is a CRO association and many companies call themselves CROs in Japan. However, CROs have not been authorized or recognized by Koseisho or the Chuikyo, the Central Social Insurance Medical Council. Instead, these companies tend to be clinical trial managers which operate as de facto employees of the manufacturer. The manufacturer maintains bottom-line responsibility for the validity of the research and its methodology.

- We believe that Koseisho is hesitant to approve CROs for fear that the pharmaceutical and medical device manufacturers will not take responsibility. There may be an enticement for the technology holder to put undue pressure on the CRO to deliver the expected results. The combination of buffering the manufacturer and commercial aspirations of companies in a country which does not have enforceable Good Clinical Practices (GCP) programs could be recipe for disaster in a system already shaken by scandal.

- When entering into an agreement with a CRO or an in-country caretaker, there are several ways a company can protect itself:

1) Contracts are very difficult to enforce midstream in any regulatory process. The CRO or in-country caretaker hold too many key cards. If they quit, the technology holder will typically have to start over, losing valuable time to market and perhaps, most importantly, its reputation in the marketplace. Even while saying this, it is important to protect yourself contractually. Clauses may include: a) *Cost containment.* Unexpected costs can always be expected in a clinical trial situation; b) *On-time-copy clause.* The regulatory process generates mountains of paper. Having copies of all documentation transferred on a monthly basis is a good way to check up on activities and keep a keen eye on trouble points. This can be a lifesaver in the event of a change in caretakers; c) *Switch-any-time clause.* A company should always have an alternative ready and be ready to enforce the clause.

2) It may be worth the extra money to employ a Western company, because of greater peace of mind and, possibly, greater transparency.

3) There are some small reputable in-country caretakers in Japan. Often they are one-man shops with limited capacity. But they can be a good choice. The key is having references.

12

John Gets Tough With Morikawa

It was a chilly day in Tokyo, but nothing compared to the weather conditions inside the Morikawa headquarters. Unlike previous occasions when someone would have greeted John in the reception area, this time John was left waiting for a considerable amount of time, long enough for even a foreigner like John to unmistakably know that he was being chastised. Finally, the telephone rang at the receptionist's desk and John was ushered into the conference room by the OL, or "office lady," dressed in a non-descript blue suit.

The Morikawa people were already in the room. There were eight persons present, with the company president himself seated in the center position of the long conference table. The faces were stone-cold impassive. There was no eye contact whatsoever. John smiled and lifted his hand in greeting and tried to make at least a flicker of eye contact with Goro, but he would have none of it and continued staring at some point in middle space. Only one chair was left unoccupied at the far end of the table and John took it. Once he had sat down, John took a moment to take stock of the circumstances. It was very odd. The drapes had been pulled in the conference room, with no outside light reaching what was, even under normal circumstances, a gloomy, dark paneled room. The room was wrapped in a blue veil of cigarette smoke—nothing unusual there. But John could feel the hostility—it was palpable.

No one seemed authorized to break the silence. Finally, after an interminable time, a Morikawa corporate warrior cut loose with the opening salvo. He was a fat guy; John thought his name might be Okamoto, Morikawa's corporate attorney. "Well, John, what do you have to say for yourself now that you have been caught red-handed in such a deceitful action?"

No doubt about it, Morikawa had succeeded in their attempt to intimidate him, John thought. For a flashing moment, John actually wondered whether he would ever leave the building alive. John caught his breath and told himself that these were penile implant distributors, not gun-carrying *yakuza* thugs. Old man Morikawa looked a bit like a Japanese version of Edward G. Robinson. Pure silence. Finally, John got the nerve to speak. He said, "I'm very sorry."

The mood of the room shifted. For the first time, the Morikawa warriors looked up and glanced at one another. They sensed victory. John felt more than saw Morikawa's razor-thin grin grow from the corners of his mouth. He seemed to puff up with his victory as he delivered the *coup d' grace*. "I assume we will have none of this kind of behavior in the future?" Morikawa said with a menacing forcefulness, pointing two fingers at John.

Oddly enough, John felt his confidence begin to grow in the face of these bullying tactics. Morikawa was beginning to stand when John stopped him in mid-rise. "I'm very sorry—that I did not tell you what I was doing. That was wrong. But, I am not sorry for getting the *shon-in* for our products."

Morikawa seemed frozen in mid-air with his butt six inches off the chair, then fell back with a soft plop. The entire room began making those odd, sucking noises.

The chilly temperatures dropped into blizzard conditions. Frightened to death when walking in, John now began to enjoy the entire drama unfolding here. What the hell! His career was on the line as was MTI's entire Japan business. He didn't want to lose his job or the Japan business, but John understood the situation well enough to know that he could lose them both anyway. Morikawa also had something at stake here. They didn't want to lose a three or four million U.S. per year profit either.

John hesitated for only a moment and then decided to take the biggest gamble of his entire life. He stood up and placed his hands on the table and then announced in a neutral tone of voice, "It appears obvious to me that events have caused too much damage to our relationship to continue. I think it is best if we cancel the distribution contract immediately and go our separate ways. Morikawa-san, I will have Big Ed telephone you to make the final arrangements."

John stared straight ahead during his speech for fear of making eye contact and breaking down. Once he finished, though, he immediately sensed that his gamble had at least a chance to pay off. Finally, he dared a glance.

Okamoto looked like a carp ready for filleting, his mouth opening and closing. Goro looked to be close to fainting, he was so pale. The veins in Morikawa's neck were standing out like guitar strings. The others simply sat, dumbfounded.

John turned to leave, hoping against hope that somehow the situation could be salvaged. His hand touched the door knob, with no sound behind him. "Please, say something," a voice in his brain screamed. "Anything. You can't let me just walk out like this!"

But nothing was said. John closed the door to the conference room and stepped into a exciting but lonely new world. He ran down the hall past the receptionist and jumped into the open elevator. He felt sick. When the doors finally opened on the first floor, John heaved on the threshold and then ran from the building.

The elevator filled with Morikawa OLs, none of them saying anything.

John's Lessons

- It is hard to bluff in meetings in corporate Japan. Typically, all possible scenarios have been discussed ad nauseam and a general consensus reached. When the outlandish occurs, an individual will be hesitant to make an on-the-spot decision for fear of breaching the consensus.

- A strong or unexpected statement should always be followed by a period of discussion. John should have said something to the effect that because this is a very big issue, please discuss it among yourselves and we can discuss it later. It need not be an extended period of time. Often a short period of ten to twenty minutes is enough to get at least a sense of the reaction.

- It is not considered impolite to whisper to one's colleagues in group discussions. If John would have just sat silently after making his statement for as long as necessary, letting the Japanese participants whisper, dialog could have continued.

13

John Wanders Tokyo in a Daze

Once outside of the Morikawa building, John cycled through a wide variety of emotions and physical sensations. First, there was embarrassment at losing his breakfast in his run from the elevator. Next, was an odd sense of elation as John remembered his gritty performance in the Morikawa board room. The elation was short-lived, however, as John recalled that he had thrown six million dollar's worth of MTI business into the pot and he hadn't even been around when people turned over their cards. From depression it was a fast ride down into near-suicidal despondency. He felt physically and mentally numb. For the merest flash of an instant John contemplated taking an elevator to the top of a building and throwing himself off.

He snapped out of that in a hurry. Come on, it wasn't the end of the world. Besides, the glimpse of Hitomi collecting all of his worldly possessions was a bracing tonic, like a couple of bottles of Lipovitan D and a kick in the ass.

OK, so it wasn't the end of the world. But he wasn't feeling real dandy either. John realized that he was leaning against a railing on a busy street near Tokyo station, almost panting in the melting heat of a mid-summer's day in Japan. There was no way he was going to go back to the office today. The sight of the chirpy and cheerful Miss Bamba was more than he could possibly stomach. Nor did he want to see any of his business acquaintances. The next realization seared John's already scarred psyche: basically, he didn't have any friends in a city of twenty-six million people. He had met hundreds of people in the past year in Japan, but all of them were related to his business. He had devoted almost every minute of his time (subtracting a bit for his initial infatuation with Hitomi) to building MTI's business in Japan. With a keen bitterness, John realized that he had literally forfeited a personal life for MTI. Somehow, it didn't seem like a great bargain.

Where to go? It was late afternoon, so John decided to simply step into the streaming flow of people and let it take him to the nearest train station. It was Tokyo station, with one million people coming and going every day. He desperately wanted a drink, but he wanted to avoid anyone who might recognize him. What better place than the Golden Gai, a warren of tiny bars in ramshackle huts near Kabukicho in Shinjuku. John remembered it from his previous time in Tokyo as a funky place with writers and other non-business types intent on staying outside of the mainstream. The area was fast disappearing, even then, as modern Tokyo encroached on the remnants of an older, more leisurely place. He hoped it was still there as he was shoved out of the orange train at Shinjuku Station by a swarming mass of sweating commuters.

Finding Kabukicho was no problem—he simply stepped into the moving flow of people and was carried to its bright lights and sleazy environs. When in doubt, ask a policeman, John thought. He found a *koban* police kiosk near the entrance to Kabukicho and asked for the Golden Gai in passable Japanese. The cop did a double take when he saw the white face and round eyes, but grunted a response and pointed in the direction of the new City Hall. John found it OK and nostalgically wandered the maze of bars, looking for the right one to drown his sorrows and help him forget his loss. He picked one particularly nondescript bar called Tsukimi or "Moon-Viewing" and walked in. It was perfect. Dirty, smelly, and totally anonymous. The bartender looked to be in his seventies at least, but he was smiling a welcome. John ordered a beer, then another and another. He was vaguely aware of people around him laughing, drinking and smoking. But he ignored them and kept on drinking until he laid his head on the counter and faded into oblivion.

He woke up around 2:00 a.m., with the old geezer shaking his arm gently and still smiling. John got the message and pulled out his wallet to pay. Very bad news. He had just enough cash to pay the bill. He had canceled his credit cards to protect himself from Hitomi's revenge and John was pretty sure that Tsukimi wasn't exactly the kind of place to take a personal check. That left him with 174 yen in change and seven hours to kill until the ATMs opened at 9:00 a.m. the next morning. That is, unless he wanted to cuddle up with Hitomi and the Jamaican duo in his expensive Tokyo apartment. Given that choice, John headed off for Shinjuku Station, determined to find a bench until the sun rose.

Shuffling to the station, John was stunned to see hundreds of homeless gathered around the vicinity. Many had constructed cardboard homes. Some were real works of art, while others were simply flattened boxes. There was an overpowering smell of urine in the hot, humid summer's night. John looked for an open spot, found one and laid down, desperate for some sleep.

He was not alone long. Shortly after closing his eyes, a delegation of three homeless came over to John and gently massaged his shoulder. He looked up at the smiling trio who clearly did not want him there. Confused at first, John grew annoyed at their interruption. "Damn. I can't even sleep on the street here. Where am I supposed to go now," he thought and showed his annoyance.

They stepped back. Noting his displeasure, the delegation began a pantomime. They obviously assumed that he could not speak Japanese. When John began barking at them in decent Japanese, they jumped back in utter disbelief. They huddled for a moment. One of them then announced to John in very polite Japanese that he was sleeping in the designated toilet.

Moments later, John found himself installed as the honored guest in one of the larger cardboard villas. They gave him a "clean" shirt to replace the urine-soaked one he had been wearing and gave him a piping hot cup of tea. They were very pleased at the prospect of having an American move into the neighborhood. Location, location, location, John guessed. And very disappointed to learn that John's stay was only temporary. Still, they sat and talked most of the night.

John learned a great deal. The homeless had their own unofficial government. They held meetings and decided where each person's sleeping area was. They had meetings with the police to decide where they could set up camp and what time to take the boxes down and even when the next raid was to be held, so that everyone could be prepared. John learned that most of the men were employed and sent the money back home to their families in the country who were experiencing very hard times. *Dekasegi* was the word they used.

And, of course, John learned that they even decided where to pee.

John's Lessons

- The most obvious point of note is the proclivity Japanese people have for forming groups and vertical hierarchies. This extends to every facet of life, including *kojiki*, or beggars, in Japan. *Kojiki* tend to adopt a similar look and exist as part of a group.

- Another important point to note is that Japanese society contains multiple levels of contradiction. For example, mobsters are "unionized" and sometimes hold massive demonstrations. But, in such an event, they either inform or ask permission of the police as to when and where such demonstrations can be held.

14

John and the Morning After

John walked the six miles or so to a bank near his capsule hotel and stepped into the bank's ATM room at exactly 9:00 a.m. for a cash withdrawal. Sweet cash, John thought. Money could be such a wonderful thing. He then bee-lined his way to the capsule hotel, where he jumped into the bath and scrubbed off every trace of his Shinjuku experience. His next stop was a noodle shop across the street and a quick slurp of ramen to get the day off on the right foot.

The last stop was his office. Even Miss Bamba was less than her usual chirpy self that morning. John knew that Goro-san probably had an inside track to MTI's affairs through Bamba-san and maybe she knew about his public disgrace the day before. Still, she said nothing about it. John noticed that silence on controversial topics seemed to be something of a trend in Japan.

John may have experienced some kind of hell the night before, but he realized that he was simply back where he started yesterday when he ran heaving from the Morikawa elevator. He had to face the music and he might as well start the symphony right now. He picked up the phone and dialed Big Ed's direct number. Waiting for a response, John checked off his list of things-to-do: close apartment, buy airline tickets, write resume, find some employment counseling, etc. That part was easy. John got a bit queasy wondering if MTI might actually try to sue him for screwing up the penile implant market in Japan and throwing away three million dollar's worth of annual sales. The noodles began to threaten moving up his esophageal tract when John heard Big Ed come on the line.

"Ed, John here in Tokyo."

"You sonofabitch," Big Ed shouted into the phone. "Where have you been? We've been trying to reach you all day. Was your phone number changed? We kept getting these guys saying 'yeah' and 'cool man.'"

"Um, it's a long story," John mumbled into the receiver. "I don't know what to say."

"Well, I know what to say. Congratulations! You finally grew some balls," Big Ed's voice blasted over the line.

Hanging up the phone a few minutes later, John broke out in nearly hysterical laughter. Big Ed was elated with his gamble. Right after the "Gunfight at the OK Corral," Morikawa himself had called MTI to complain bitterly about John's actions and demanded that he be removed from Japan at once. Big Ed told him to "bite his big one" and hung up. John broke out laughing again at the image of the Morikawa staff poring over English-Japanese dictionaries to find out the exact meaning of the colloquial term "bite the big one." No doubt they got the point, if not the nuance.

For a couple of moments John debated whether to take the day off and spend a day recuperating from the barrage of physical and psychological blows that he had absorbed in the past few days. But he quickly turned off those thoughts when he realized that he had the ball and an open field in front of him. Now was the time to turn it on. His instructions from Big Ed were very clear. The first order of business was to develop a business plan for Japan that would turn MTI from a victim to a champion as soon as possible. That meant creating a complete business, marketing, and regulatory plan for Japan. Even more, it meant implementing that plan. The one thing that Big Ed said that gave John pause was his comment, "No more fuck-ups. This is it. Next time, you call me with something off-plan, you'd better have your bags packed for Siberia."

But Big Ed had given him a blank check of sorts. "It will take time and money, but let's do it right this time."

The total shocker was that John was promoted to Vice President,

Japan Operations. It had a nice ring to it. Much better than unemployment. John was still quasi-euphoric when he walked up to his best "friend," Kashiwagi-san, the desk attendant at the Royal Kanda Capsule Hotel. John felt totally drained and wanted nothing more than to strip off his clothes and jump into the water with his chinpira pals. But, Kashiwagi-san pointed behind John and turned around. There was a very distraught looking Goro-san, slumped on the brown vinyl couch. John was stunned to see him.

"John, we must talk," Goro-san pleaded.

"I'm listening, but you're going to have to talk to me in the bath."

Goro-san turned up the pleading dial a couple of notches. "We can work this out. It's all a big misunderstanding."

John stopped with one foot in the bath and said, "Goro-san, there's no misunderstanding. MTI and Morikawa have been heading toward this collision for years. It's over."

Goro-san cranked the dial all the way up. "But I will have to take responsibility for all of this. I will have to take the blame. I'll become a *madogiwa*." There were tears in his eyes and looked like he could use MTI's deluxe model SKU #14-5B at that point.

MTI's new Vice President of Japan Operations took a careful look at Goro-san and stepped completely into the bath. "I'm sorry for you personally, but there's no turning back now. If you need a job, call me. But, let me tell you one thing man-to-man. If you call me, you'd better have the MTI customer and distributor lists." With that, John sat down in the bath, folded his towel on top of his head and gave himself up to one of Japan's great pleasures.

John's Lessons

- It often takes a crisis to make partners come to grips with the true reality of their relationship.

- Lifetime employment is under pressure from every direction in Japan. But the concept of loyalty to a company is still an extremely powerful force in Japan and one that can be easily manipulated by management.

15

John Bucks the Power Brokers

The entire office was a shambles. The floor was covered with books, papers, computer peripherals, everything. Even the metal filing cabinets had been pried open and the contents strewn everywhere. John stared at the carnage in disbelief. Why? Who? It just made no sense in a place like Japan.

He walked carefully through the office, trying to step over and around the garbage and overturned chairs. Even his prized Fijian cannibal fork was shattered. Numb, John made his way to the product storeroom and pushed open the slightly ajar door. It didn't give at first. He pushed again harder and managed to push it open enough to see inside. Shock turned to blind rage. The new shipment of penile implants had been ripped out of the boxes and vandalized. John bent down and picked up a few samples and realized that they had been slashed, with the sensors ripped from the tips and the silicon exteriors torn and gaping.

Finally, ugly reality forced its way through his numbness. All of MTI's clinical samples were ... gone... and the urology show was just two days away.

Turning from the mess, John heard a soft noise from the closed door of the conference room. He covered the ten yards as quickly as he could and flung open the door and hit the light switch. There he saw old Komatsu-san, the building janitor, cowering in the corner. Five feet tall and seventy if a day, Komatsu came in every morning to clean the toilets and empty the garbage. John reached over and grabbed him by his jacket lapels and shouted at him in the most guttural Japanese that his *chinpira* buds could have mustered. "Tell me!" He picked him up off his feet and started shaking him violently from side to side. "Who did this?"

Komatsu-san had been friendly to John, quick to say *Ohayo gozaimasu* in the mornings and *Otsukaresama deshita* at night when John left the building. But all John could see was an object on which to vent his own rage. He started to put Komatsu-san down, realizing that he was just a helpless victim caught in a bad situation. But something odd struck John about his demeanor—he wasn't protesting. In fact, he kept whimpering and apologizing. Apologizing? John couldn't figure it out.

Finally, it struck John that this helpless victim was in fact an accessory to the crime. He jerked him off his feet again, this time rage mixed with a particularly bitter sense of betrayal. "Who did it? Why did you let them in? Tell me, or I'll throw you out the window."

Komatsu-san had never been known as a particularly brave man by his wife and friends and, looking into the face of a crazed barbarian fully one-foot taller than him, Komatsu quickly decided it was not time to turn over a new leaf. He broke down. "I'm so sorry, John-san. You've always been nice to me. They said they only wanted to look around. There were three of them. They gave me some money. I'm sorry—I don't want the money. I'm so ashamed. *Gomen nasai.*"

John's entire demeanor changed. It wasn't Komatsu's fault. He let him down carefully. Then he did the unexpected to Komatsu. He forgave the little caretaker. "It's OK, Komatsu-san. I know you didn't mean to do this. Everything is insured. It can be replaced," John lied, thinking about his files and the damaged products. "I just need to know who did this. Who were the men?"

Komatsu began whimpering again. "I can't tell you. You'll tell the police and they'll arrest me."

John sighed heavily. His office had just been trashed and now he was trying to reassure the person who'd allowed it to happen, instead of heaving him out of the window like he deserved. "Don't worry. I'll tell you what. I have to call the police. But you can just tell them that you don't know what happened and didn't see anything. But I need to know. No one will know that you told me."

"But I'm the only one besides you with a key."

"Exactly. I'll tell the police that I mistakenly left the door open last night and failed to set the security. It was an honest mistake."

Komatsu began whimpering and trembling at the same time. "There were three of them. They didn't tell me who they were. They gave me fifty-thousand yen and told me to get lost. I went around the corner. I don't think they knew I was still there. I'm not sure, but I heard one of them they say something about a Morisawa-san. Does that mean anything?"

"Morisawa-san?" John sat down hard on one of the conference room chairs. "They said Morisawa?" Very softly, John asked him, "Could it possibly have been Morikawa-san that you heard?"

Seeing John's reaction, Komatsu started wringing his hands. "Yes, I think maybe it was. I'm so sorry. Please forgive me."

John stared at the wall for a few moments. Finally, he nodded toward the door and snapped in colloquial English, "Get out of here."

Komatsu didn't speak English, but he got the message clearly and vanished.

John's first call wasn't to the police, it was to Bruce. It was almost 9:00 a.m. and Miss Bamba would be there any minute. He figured that she could handle the immediate unpleasant task of dealing with the police on this matter.

He needed a different kind of help. For the first time, John thought about Big Ed and his first commandment, "Thou shalt not fuck up again." John knew that he needed to prove that Morikawa was some-how behind this or else MTI's new Vice President of Japan Operations would be sleeping again with the homeless in Shinjuku.

Bruce didn't know it yet, but he was going to add detective work to his menu of consulting options.

Three days later John met Bruce at a favorite place in the Azabu Juban area of central Tokyo. Earlier in the day Bruce had called John and said that he had learned information that John needed to know right away. They were the only customers in the red-lantern pub with its old timbers stretched above their heads stained with decades of oil and smoke. Once the obligatory beers were ordered and an initial order of grilled chicken, Bruce got down to the details of an amazing story.

"Your janitor heard it right. It was Morikawa."

John blanched. For three days he had been hoping that Komatsu was wrong and that MTI was somehow the victim of a random vandalizing. He took a big gulp of beer and asked Bruce to continue.

"Do you know a company called PenilePro?" John nodded. "Well, Morikawa signed a secret exclusive agreement with them soon after your little scene in the Morikawa boardroom. The word on the street is that Morikawa is frantically going through the *shonin* process to beat MTI to the punch. I learned that they have stockpiled a year's worth of products and they plan to convert all of MTI's customers to PenilePro. It seems their strategy to destroy MTI has two main objectives. First, they wanted to destroy your *shonin* documentation, hence the trashing of your office. Second, they are forking over huge amounts of money to Dr. Tani to stonewall MTI in Koseisho."

John stared openmouthed at Bruce through the entire dissertation. Even in his worst moment John could not have imagined that things were this bad. "How could you ever have learned all of this? This is too outlandish, even for Morikawa."

It was obvious that Bruce was preparing John for the moment of truth. He nodded to the sliding door of the smoky pub and the last person on earth that John expected to see pushed aside the rope curtain and entered room. It was Goro-san.

It took three large beers before Goro-san became inebriated enough to divulge the inside story of Morikawa's revenge. The story was something out of a TV drama. Apparently, Morikawa had gone berserk when he found out what "big one" Big Ed had told him to bite. That, combined with the fact Morikawa was faced with closing their medical distribution business without the MTI product line had created a highly flammable mixture of personal outrage and economic vulnerability.

Using their lawyer's underworld connections, Morikawa hired the three *chinpira* to trash the MTI office and destroy their products and steal the regulatory documentation that MTI would need to submit for their own *shonin*. They succeeded in destroying the products, but they never found the regulatory materials.

John stopped Goro-san long enough to say that, luckily, he had just given the entire dossier to Dr. Morita at JBBD to put the final touches on the submission package to Koseisho. Still, the damage was extensive.

John stared at Goro-san and asked, "Where do you stand now?"

Goro-san stared down at the table, unwilling to make eye contact with John, and asked if his offer to join MTI was still valid. He had already tendered his resignation to Morikawa and had nowhere else to go.

John sighed and took a gulp of beer, feeling both the pressure of betrayal and the desire to make someone pay for it. Then he remembered that Big Ed had given him another chance. He figured it was time to pay back that favor to someone else. "OK, you're on board. But I want your total loyalty. If I tell you to slice your belly with a bamboo sword your only response will be *'Hai.'*"

"Hai," responded Goro-san.

The next morning Bruce and Goro-san joined John in the MTI conference room to plan damage control and their next steps to counter Morikawa's offensive.

Bruce began the deliberations. "Desperate times call for decisive action." For the next two hours Bruce and Goro-san outlined a series of innovative and risky actions that left John shaking his head.

Bruce led the way. "First, you need to understand the current situation of scandals that have been rocking Koseisho and Japan's medical world. We have the Nihon Shoji scandal in which the Dr. Tani of that group doctored clinical results on behalf of the manufacturer. That little misstep resulted in six dead, that we know of."

Goro-san stepped in. "Next, we have the Green Cross HIV scandal in which Green Cross executives colluded with Koseisho officials to keep dangerous unheated blood products on the market, even though safe products were available from a foreign manufacturer. These are not nice men. Green Cross was begun by "scientists" from the notorious Unit 731 that performed vivisection experiments on people in

Manchuria during World War II. That collusion has resulted in Japan's entire hemophiliac population becoming at risk for HIV. There are about 5,000 hemophiliacs in Japan, 1,800 of whom are confirmed positive. Already 400 of them are dead and the others are just waiting for the worst."

It was like tag-team wrestling. When Goro-san finished, Bruce jumped into the ring. "These examples are just the ones we know about. Given the medical world's penchant for quietly burying its mistakes, there could be thousands of people and families who have had their lives destroyed by Japan's "power broker" system. If we knew the real score, the entire society would be shocked."

He continued. "The good news is that the new head of Koseisho genuinely appears to want to change the system. Heads are already beginning to roll."

Goro-san jumped back in. "The Japanese public has finally gotten involved. The newspapers and weekly magazines are full of stories about what's happening in the medical world. There's a growing concern about the entire system. People are beginning to ask for a more transparent system and an end to these power brokers who think nothing of building their careers on the mistakes and suffering of their patients. We're even beginning to see the a demand for the type of informed consent that you take for granted in the United States."

"OK, OK." John held up his hand. "I get the picture. But I need more than a list of recent medical scandals when I talk to Big Ed next time. What's the take-away message here for MTI?"

Both Goro and Bruce looked at each other and said in unison, "Science."

"Science?" John queried.

"Science," Bruce explained. "A clinical trial and entire *shonin* application based strictly on carefully documented and regulated scientific method."

John found himself automatically shaking his head. A year of hitting his head against the brick wall of Japan's medical practices had bred a knee-jerk cynicism about this possibility. It seemed farfetched. But maybe, just maybe, it could work. Once again, John thought, he had precious little to lose. Why not raise the stakes and gamble that MTI could contribute to a much-needed change in Japan. And, if it worked...

Two days later John found himself in a secluded *ryotei*, a high-class restaurant in the high-rent district of Akasaka, a place famous for its late night meetings between Japan's most powerful men secretly plotting their paths to power. Totally inconspicuous on the outside, the *ryotei* interior exuded that understated elegance which marks one of Japan's great contributions to world culture. Given the topic under discussion, the place was perfect. Joining John was Dr. Morita, who served as the go-between for this meeting with a young, up-and-coming urology researcher.

Dr. Suzuki was forty-three years old. He had an M.D. from one of Japan's most prestigious universities and a Ph.D. from the University of Pittsburgh, the same school where Dr. Tani studied and launched Japan's entry into the exciting world of penile implant technology. He was part of Dr. Tani's *gakubatsu*, or university group. Dr. Suzuki was one of several promising young professors who was battling in secret to take on Dr. Tani's mantle as "power broker" in the field when Dr. Tani stepped down in ten years or so.

Sweat dripped from Dr. Suzuki's forehead, despite the near-frigid atmosphere in the *ryotei*. Even his hand shook as he held his glass of beer. Simply meeting with them was a hugely dangerous step for Dr. Suzuki, Dr. Morita had informed John prior to the meeting.

"That's unthinkable!" Dr. Suzuki said automatically after a mere moment of thought. "We must go through Dr. Tani to perform this clinical trial. Without him we could never get Koseisho approval for this product."

"We think that conditions are changing in Japan," Dr. Morita replied in a soft, reasonable tone of voice, glancing side to side to make sure that no one was eavesdropping. "The age of the power broker is coming to an end. Either we change with the world or we'll be left behind. In the end, science must dictate our actions, not personal influence or political actions."

Dr. Suzuki looked at the tatami mat next to the low table. A powerful battle seemed to be underway inside of him. From what John had heard about Dr. Suzuki, it was a battle between huge personal ambition and, judging from the drop of sweat hanging so tantalizingly from the tip of his nose, fear.

Finally, Dr. Suzuki spoke. His first words evidenced the side of personal ambition. "I've forgotten more about penile implants than Dr. Tani has ever known." He turned red with embarrassment when he realized how blatantly honest he had been in his self-assessment.

"That is why we are talking to you," John said in what he hoped was a soothing and reassuring voice. "Koseisho wants a change. The Japanese people want a change. Young academic and clinical researchers like you want a change. That change could start with you. I want you to manage one of our clinical trials. I want you to base your trial strictly on science, with no thought of the politics and no thought of money. Of course, you will be able to publish any findings and the results of the paper will be completely up to you."

Dr. Suzuki looked at John. The battle was waging more furiously than before. This time fear came to the fore. "What if things don't change? Where will I be then? My family will be disgraced. My career will be over. My position as secretary of the *gakkai* will be taken away. I would be a dead man walking."

Dr. Morita and John exchanged glances. Everything Dr. Suzuki had said was absolutely true. There was no point in downplaying the truth. Dr. Suzuki would see through any deception in an instant. John decided to meet Dr. Suzuki's fears head on. "Yes. Your career would be over. But, if it does change, you will be famous in the medical community. You will have the honor and prestige of a doctor like Sugita Gempaku, a man who literally risked his life to bring better medicine to the people of Japan."

John's words had hit the mark. Dr. Suzuki clearly saw himself in the mold of a great doctor. They were at the moment of truth. The forces of ambition and fear were in locked in a death struggle inside of the young doctor.

John tried his last gambit. "Doctor, you know that we're right. Japan must change. It must take its place in the scientific community."

Dr. Suzuki turned to Dr. Morita. "If I do this, what is your honest opinion of our chances of success?"

Dr. Morita took a deep breath and responded in a very low, serious tone of voice. "Maybe ten percent. Best case, twenty percent."

Silence gripped the table. It was a moment of truth for a man, a moment when he decided the quality of his life and his contribution to the world. Fear won. Dr. Suzuki bowed his head and placed his hands on the table. "I am sorry. I know that you are right. Japan must change. But if I fail, I will have nowhere to go. The risk is too high." With that, Dr. Suzuki stood up, bowed again and quickly left the room.

Dr. Morita and John said nothing, each lost in his own thoughts. Although bitterly disappointed, John could not find it in his heart to blame Dr. Suzuki for his choice. The magnitude of his battle was the measure of their challenge. John recalled Sugita Gempaku's words about having surmounted insurmountable obstacles and he knew that more than anything else he wanted to know the joy of making that kind of difference.

"We'll just keep looking until we find the right man," he said. Dr. Morita nodded.

John's Lessons

- Virtually every member of the scientific community is aware of the weaknesses of the Japanese system. They understand that science is often a victim of this structure and it is a source of keen regret. But the system has a life of its own, and the researcher who tries to single-handedly rebel can be annihilated by the following structures:

1) *The University Group System.* Japan's most prestigious medical universities have created vertical ties between researchers throughout the country. Once researchers or physicians are identified as members of one of these groups, they are essentially stuck with that label for their entire career.

2) *University Group Leaders.* The leader of each of these vertical university groups is usually the survivor of an intense political struggle. They are very smart men and at one time they probably demonstrated strong technical abilities. But at some point they made a decision to focus on politics over science and there is not enough time in the

day to do both well. The leaders often have absolute power over researchers and physicians. They are masters of their universe. They can be skillful supporters or brutal adversaries.

The most powerful constraint on any Japanese researcher or physician is that there is no escape from the system if they criticize their superior or somehow transgress. Being fired is not the ultimate humiliation. Instead, Japanese fear isolation and remoteness more than loss of employment. Because of the power of vertical groups, there is no way to step across the boundary to another vertical group. Needless to say, this scenario is not conducive to the free exchange of information and the risk-taking that is necessary for cutting-edge science.

However, Japan in its inimitable way has devised an often effective method to overcome this huge obstacle. Although the *tatemae* is that the power brokers possess absolute power, the reality is that Japan's real thought leaders in the medical profession are the mid-career associate professors at leading university hospitals. In the guise of serving their masters, these men (and occasionally women) perform the actual research and publish the papers. Of course, the name of the power broker is most prominently displayed and the power broker will give the keynote speech at the *gakkai* meeting. But everyone in the room knows the *honne* of the situation and will pay respect to the person who did the work, unless he or she belongs to a different university group (in which case fear and backbiting are more typical responses).

16

Tragedy Strikes John's Clinical Trials

It took several weeks and countless interviews but John and Dr. Morita were convinced that they had finally found their man, or in this case, men. Dr. Doi and Dr. Sakai sat side-by-side in the MTI conference room. Both were in their mid-thirties and associate professors at good universities.

Within ten minutes John knew with crystal clarity that Dr. Doi was a certifiable genius. He was articulate, creative, and had a complete grasp of the entire field of penile implants in Japan and the world. With equal clarity, John also knew why Dr. Doi would never make it to power broker status in Japan. His father had worked for one of Japan's huge trading companies and Dr. Doi had attended American schools from the fifth to the ninth grades. He was smart enough to graduate from the best of Japan's universities and medical schools, but he was a very square peg in a round hole society. For relaxation, Dr. Doi liked to play guitar in a band that played Bob Dylan songs at live music clubs and play Frisbee with his dog. That alone would probably have marked him as an eccentric in Japan, but what placed him firmly in the untouchable category was his penchant for debate with his elders, particularly about the practice of medicine. This was an American virus he had apparently caught during his stay in America and the Japanese response was to quarantine him. He had embarrassed too many of his superiors to ever have the quarantine lifted.

Dr. Doi was a goner and he knew it. His days were non-stop surgeries. He was too good to ignore, but his superiors felt that the best way to keep him out of trouble and out of their way was to keep him very busy. He was unabashedly excited about the opportunity sitting on the other side of the conference table. Unlike Dr. Suzuki, Dr. Doi had nothing to lose. Personal ambition would win the battle and the war without a struggle.

Dr. Sakai fit another category altogether. He was the complete insider, taking the "escalator" from kindergarten to university and medical school at Keio University, Japan's most famous private medical school. The inside word on Dr. Sakai was that he was technically competent, but no genius.

He was also much more nervous about the entire situation than Dr. Doi. After a few minutes of conversation with him, John got the impression that he still believed that he had a chance to make it inside the current system. He craved the respect of his peers which he believed had been unfairly withheld from him. Dr. Sakai's tragedy was that his mentor was caught in a squalid internal scandal and forced to resign. That left Dr. Sakai twisting in the wind, unsupported by the all-important mentor. As an insider and a victim of the system, Dr. Sakai was a man for whom most felt pity, but was untouchable nonetheless. His only hope of fulfilling his dreams of respect and power lay across the table. He was not particularly optimistic about his chances nor particularly motivated by the idealism of changing a bad system. He simply wanted to step off the assembly line of surgeries and move out of the back row at medical meetings.

Dr. Sakai was first to speak. "John-san, the design of your study was very interesting. I especially liked the double blind, dual structure of the study." He paused and looked at Dr. Doi. "But Dr. Doi and I have some disagreement and I am sure you can set things straight."

John replied, curious to understand the differences. "As I said the conduct of the study should be up to you two. My only requirement is that it must be based on impeccable science."

"Yes, of course." Dr. Sakai responded excitedly. The mole on his chin was twitching, side to side. "I agree that we should only use impeccable scientific methods. But we also need to agree to informal discussions. You know... between professionals."

"I don't think I understand," John said, perplexed. He glanced at Dr. Doi, who was smiling condescendingly.

"It is just that Dr. Doi told me that he will not have any contact with me during the study and will not collaborate until after all the data has been tabulated." Dr. Sakai was fidgeting nervously, his mole still bouncing around. John wondered how he did that. "It sounds reasonable to me. What's the problem?"

"What do we do if the data varies significantly? There could be procedural differences. Differences in interpretation of data anomalies. A host of things could go wrong. It would be scientifically unsound to conduct a double-blind study without at least informal collaboration between dedicated professionals." His voice rose in tone and intensity.

Dr. Doi had had enough. John could easily understand how he managed to upset people left and right. "Collaborating, as you call it is a violation of scientific method! Not only will I not "collaborate" as you put it, I will not allow the data out of my hands. It will not be available to any of my technicians. Laboratory work will be submitted by code, to be known only to me and all clinical case cards will be only done by me and kept in a safe."

Clearly frustrated, Dr. Sakai said, "I only want good science, just like John has said. But I think that collaboration is the basis for good science. We especially need to collaborate at the level of clinical case cards and we need to allow our technical staff to work together! That is good cooperative clinical method. I will only participate in good clinical methods."

Dr. Doi stood up and faced the window. He seemed to be doing the professional equivalent of counting to ten.

John stepped in as the referee. "Doctors, surely there is a simple solution. We will simply rely on GCP, Good Clinical Practices, to establish all study guidelines."

Dr. Sakai's face reddened. "John-san, you've been in Japan long enough now to know the difference between *tatemae* and *honne*. GCP is *tatemae*. The *honne* here is that we must look for the truth in science together. We must cooperate!"

"Dr. Sakai," John said with as much patience as he could muster. "In many clinical studies, researchers don't even know who the other researchers are, let alone collaborate." Dr. Doi was smiling again. John glanced at him with annoyance. He clearly did not wear his brilliance easily.

Dr. Sakai continued. "But if our results are different, one of us could be wrong and the results will be published. My God, I could be humiliated!"

It was Dr. Doi's turn to speak. "It does not necessarily follow that one of us is wrong, just different. At the conclusion of the study and during tabulation of data we would collaborate in order to ascertain the reasons for discrepancies in the data. It is the very empirical objectivity of the trial design that ensures that we produce scientifically valid data. Anything less is not science. Surely, you can understand that, can't you? Our patients deserve nothing less."

John agreed totally with Dr. Doi's comments. He just wished that he had checked his arrogance at the door and given Dr. Sakai some space to back down and see the truth of it. As it stood now, Dr. Sakai could only admit his error or walk away, humiliated.

Dr. Sakai chose to walk away. His mole picked up speed. "I understand, but I just cannot expose myself to potential ridicule. I know that Dr. Doi is a better surgeon than I am. I will surely lose this contest." He stood up to leave the room. He left one comment hanging on the air, more in the way of self-confession than communication to the men sitting around the conference table. "I can't even rebel properly. I am a total failure. There's nothing left for me to do."

Three weeks later John heard from Dr. Morita that Dr. Sakai had jumped in front of a train at Hiroo station on the Hibiya Line. He left a wife and two kids, but no note. His colleagues said that his despondency had grown in intensity in the past several weeks, but no one suspected that he was contemplating suicide. But then, Dr. Sakai had always hidden his emotions from his colleagues and family.

John thought back to Dr. Sakai's poignant self-confession at their meeting on the clinical trial. He understood there was nothing he could have done to change the course of events that Dr. Sakai set in motion. But as he closed his eyes to sleep that night, John sadly wondered if Dr. Sakai wasn't really a victim of our obsessive desire to better the scientific method in Japan. How many more would there be? Would he be among them?

John Discovers the Japanese CRO

The next few weeks were grueling and dispiriting for the MTI team. Dr. Sakai's suicide weighed heavily on the group. It also made it difficult to interview other potential candidates for the study, knowing that they were risking not only the careers of well-meaning researchers, but possibly their very lives.

They reviewed the CVs of potential researchers, but it felt like they were simply spinning their wheels. Their list of things to do was growing but no progress was being made. While the regulatory approval applications for MTI's older products had been filed by the diligent Dr. Morita, the all-important first step of clinical trials for MTI's blockbuster new product had yet to be made.

Even worse, the word around town was that Morikawa was pulling ahead in the clinical trial race. A city of twenty-five million people, Tokyo was in many ways a small village where news traveled fast. MTI's "science-only" campaign had ended in a disaster and the entire industry knew about it. Everywhere John went he faced a chorus of smug "we told you so's." Their only consolation was that Morikawa had climbed into bed with PenilePro, one of MTI's relatively weak competitors, who had been virtually shut out of the American market because of the unfortunate tendency of their product to rupture, blowing out the lateral wall of the surgically-reconstructed penis. Very unfortunate for the patient, John thought, but a lucky break for MTI.

Time was a double-edged enemy for John. Morikawa was in the clinic with his competitor's products and John was beginning to sense that Big Ed's absolution on his first commandment was a grenade with the pin pulled. If John couldn't find a solution to the clinical trial problem he was going to be collateral damage.

The answer came to him late one evening when he was sitting on the train station platform. He began humming one of his favorite songs, "I Heard It through the Grapevine," by Credence Clearwater Revival. "CCR. What a group," he thought. "Hmm... CCR. Something about CCR." Then, like a flash it came to him—CRO! Clinical Research Organization. MTI had successfully utilized them both in the USA and Europe, why not Japan? Why not indeed!

Early the next morning he sat with Dr. Morita and was very pleased to find there was a list of CROs in Japan. He was familiar with several of them from his stint in the United States. There was even a Japan CRO Association. He could hardly restrain himself. This was it! The solution to his problem.

"Why didn't we do this from the beginning?" he asked himself. "We'll simply hire a CRO and let them deal with all of this. I know they'll be more expensive, but Big Ed will have to go along with it if the proposal comes from a brand-name CRO. The more he thought about it, the more excited John became.

Finally, he regained his senses and took a look at Dr. Morita, who did not appear to share his unbridled enthusiasm. In fact, he was making sucking noises. A very bad sign. By this time, John trusted Dr. Morita enough to know that what he was about to hear was not going to be anything but the unvarnished truth. "OK, what's the problem? I can take it."

"CROs are illegal in Japan," his mouth barely moving.

"Illegal? How can they be illegal? I'm holding a list of CROs doing business right here in Tokyo." John virtually barked at the poor man.

"Koseisho has not approved them yet," Morita-san said matter-of-factly.

"Well, what about this Japan CRO Association? What the hell is that?"

Dr. Morita sighed. Foreigners were so quick to react and so slow to understand. "The CRO Association is in preparation for the possible approval of CROs in Japan."

John quickly descended further into profanity. "Damn it! What do you mean the possible approval? Are you telling me that all of these companies have offices in Tokyo and they're just sitting around playing with themselves?"

Dr. Morita retained his composure, but he was inwardly thinking that Americans really are overbearing. "Of course not," he replied calmly. "They are doing clinical research."

"But you said research is illegal." John was beyond exasperation.

Dr. Morita managed a smile. "*Tatemae* and *honne*, John-san."

John now wished like hell that he had never started humming that stupid song. Lost in thought, John unwittingly started humming it again. Damn. It was time to give Bruce a call and get the inside skinny on this.

"Tell me about CROs in Japan," John asked Bruce.

Bruce was sitting at his desk, typing furiously. He ignored John's question. His eyes were glazed over and he had the slightly deranged look of a mad scientist pulling too much overtime in the lab. John had seen him this way enough times to know that all he could do was wait until Bruce was beamed back to earth. John stood up and walked back to the receptionist's desk where he started chatting with Hirai. She was Miss Bamba's clone in a very short skirt. In fact, she was beyond chirpy; she was hyper-cheerful. John stopped and drifted off into his own thoughts. "Why couldn't I have found someone like this instead of that bimbo Hitomi? It was my mistake, though. The Passion Fruit Club was probably not the best genetic pool to dive into."

Bruce finally wandered back to the reception area. "Do we have any coffee?" he asked. "John, when did you get here?"

John shook his head. "I came to ask you about CROs in Japan."

"Didn't we go through this before?"

"Maybe. But it obviously didn't connect in my brain. I'm thinking of turning our study over to a CRO and I need to know everything I can about them in Japan."

"It's a long story," Bruce said.

"I've got time."

"Well, it's also going to take some money. The clock's running."

"You're my best-paid friend. I'd expect nothing less."

Seated in the JBBD conference room, Bruce weighed in on the Japan CRO story. "There are no Japan CROs in the Western definition of the term. There are many companies which call themselves CROs, but in fact their function is both the same and different."

John wondered if maybe Bruce hadn't been in Japan too long. "Hell, Bruce, if I wanted double talk, I'd let Dr. Morita confuse me. Give me the straight stuff here, would you?"

Bruce got a bit testy. "Try listening a bit. You're paying for it. The biggest difference is that of responsibility. Only the manufacturer or licensed importer can take responsibility for the reliability of data generated during a clinical trial. Companies that call themselves CROs act on behalf of their client and then act as an employee of sorts. But the technology holder does not release responsibility for the data. The other difference is that CROs in Japan have a tendency to also prepare most documentation for submission of a *shonin* application and actually walk it through the process on behalf of the company. While no written guarantees are ever given, there is always a feeling that they are responsible to ensure that an approval is received."

Despite Bruce's admonition to listen, John couldn't help himself. "But that creates an inherent conflict of interest."

Bruce smiled. "Exactly. There are multiple layers of gentle contradiction. But nothing totally out of reason. You might try thinking of it as a pseudo-CRO system. For the company most successful in gaining approvals, the reward will be more customers. Thus giving them a huge business incentive to generate the best possible data. This, combined with vague Good Clinical Practices (GCP) requirements and lax enforcement by Koseisho and competing academic groups would be a recipe for disaster if CROs were let loose in Japan."

"So, you agree with Koseisho's stance?" John asked.

"Hell, yes! Eventually, CROs will be good for the Japanese clinical system. But in the meantime there is a pressing need to develop rules and mechanisms for enforcement. Without that structure CROs would be motivated to perform less than ideal science. Even worse, they would be the insulation between Koseisho, the legal system, pharmaceutical companies, and the Japanese population at large."

"I don't follow you. What do you mean insulation?"

"Come on, John. You've been here long enough to know that the bad guys seldom take the fall for their bad deeds. Especially if the bad guys belong to a powerful and wealthy industry like that of the pharmaceutical industry in Japan. They always find a scapegoat. Someone resigns to take responsibility and then gets appointed as an advisor to his company and nothing changes. Even by Japanese standards, the CRO would be too easy a target for scapegoating. If there were any bad results, the industry would simply point at the CRO, especially a foreign-owned CRO, and blame them for everything."

"But, Bruce, I know CROs in the United States and they go to incredible lengths to keep squeaky clean. Their credibility depends totally on generating reliable and replicatable data. In fact, their entire business depends on it. I can't believe that they would come to Japan and do anything like what you are saying."

"I couldn't agree more," Bruce said. "Foreign managers will come to Japan with high hopes and every intention of doing business in an ethical manner. Even if not for the sake of idealized ethics, they would see their business survival in terms of following the prescribed rules. The danger is that they must rely on their Japanese employees to do the groundwork and those employees will feel the entire weight of the Japanese system. Of course they will want to operate in an ethical manner, but all those wonderful Japanese terms that you've learned such as *tatemae* and *honne*, not to mention plain old fear, will wear down even the most resolute employee when the moment of truth comes. If you ever doubt it, just call up the memory of Dr. Suzuki's face as he left the room."

"So, basically, you're telling me that I can't use a CRO for our clinical trial," John said, his shoulders slumping in defeat.

"I didn't say that," Bruce retorted. "Even in their current incarnation, CROs can be utilized, if they are managed appropriately and aggressively. You need to take the following steps." Bruce stood up and started making a list on the white board.

As he wrote, John looked at the list and thought, "Man, nothing is easy in this country. On the other hand, nothing could be worse than working with the FDA on a brand new technology." Bruce's list made sense, given the context. John decided to give it a chance; it was the latest in his series of lessons.

John's Lessons

- Use a foreign-owned CRO—A subsidiary of a trusted U.S. CRO or one with close ties.

- Have the study designed initially in English by Western researchers.

- Have the study design translated into Japanese and then back into English.

- Specify that the CRO will be responsible for research only as your agent. Compensation will be based upon time and patients exiting the study on a set timetable. They will not be responsible for submission or a successful application.

- The CRO will need to go to Koseisho for administrative guidance, but all application documentation should be prepared by a different company or by your own staff.

- Your own staff should actively review all patient case cards to ensure the physicians are complying with the clinical design goals.

17

John Learns About Slimy Competition

The news from Goro-san was not good. Basically, Morikawa was kicking the hell out of them. With Dr. Tani's careful guidance, the PenilePro product was almost through the clinical trial process. Even some potentially good news had turned out to be no good. Goro-san's spy inside of Morikawa had told them about a potential disaster for Morikawa in the trial. The word was that one of the patients had experienced a lateral penile blow-out, but the data had been expunged from the trial and the patient wasn't talking. The bad news for MTI was that the patient was a fifty-two-year old married man who had his blow-out during a whoring binge in Osaka while testing out his new wings. He was just as keen as Morikawa to keep the details of his "problem" under wraps.

Regardless of Morikawa's problems, they had to push on. John and his team worked diligently with their new CRO, Tokyo Regulatory Services, to set up the study. Taking Bruce's advice, John contracted to have the basic study format drawn up in the States and had it translated, twice. It was a very instructive process. The two documents showed more differences than commonalties. Unfortunately, the third try did little to reconcile the dilemma. While the Japanese language can be used just as precisely as English, ambiguity and imprecision are commonly present as cultural accompaniments. However many drafts it took, they'd get their precise clinical document. John would not be deflected on this point.

Finally, they took their thirty-six-page masterpiece to the lead clinical trial investigator located by the pseudo-CRO, a Dr. Ono. He frowned deeply as he thumbed through the document, occasionally stopping to make a disapproving sound or two before turning the page. Finally, he made his pronouncement. "There will need to be some changes."

Dr. Morita was designated go-between. "We of course understand that you will be responsible for the final document. But we humbly request that you employ the basic format outlined in this document." Dr. Morita threw in enough *keigo,* or honorific language to make even the most ego-inflated doctor glow with the honor of it all. However, it was unthinkable that the doctor would show that the *keigo* had its effect, so he merely grunted once or twice. Finally, the dominos fell over for MTI: "I'm sure we will have a satisfactory outcome."

John felt like giving up. The entire process seemed to be a scene from a Kafka novel. It was in the hands of the CRO now. Standing on the train platform at Ochanomizu Station waiting for the train back to the office, he turned to Dr. Morita and asked, "What can we do now?"

As the train pulled to a stop and they stepped onto the train, Dr. Morita did his best to sum things up in a positive way. "The only thing we can do is monitor everything closely. We have been assured access to all patient case cards, all laboratory results, and we have the right to visit the patients both before and after their operations. We can also directly interview any patient we wish for five years after the procedure. That is all we can do, John-san. We cannot dictate how the investigator will perform. We are now spectators."

John sighed with the frustration of it all as he watched Tokyo flash by the train windows. Their attempt to impose pure, unadulterated science had failed. But at least they had instituted a wide variety of fail-safe mechanisms to ensure the safety of the patients and the veracity of the clinical data. John would pull the pin on the entire trial before he would compromise on those two points.

The next week they received Dr. Ono's new version of the MTI Clinical Trial Plan. It was twenty-one pages long.

John took the call from Goro-san over the intercom early on Monday morning. Even with his cellular phone barely holding the connection,

John could tell that the placid Goro-san was excited, so much so that he wasn't making any sense. "It's all over. *Shimatta, yo!*"

"Whoa. Take it easy. What's over?" John's first thought was that Dr. Ono had changed his mind and kicked out their clinical plan. Goro-san's cellular kicked back in.

"They've pulled the trial."

John felt queasy thinking about the months of hard work and sweat they had all poured into getting this bastard off the ground. They had enrolled three patients and the results had been first-rate. Why in the hell would they pull the trial now? Queasiness slipped into full-fledged nausea.

Goro-san's next words turned John's world on its head. "Morikawa. They pulled the trial."

John's heart leaped. "Morikawa?"

Goro-san's connection was now crystal clear and he had calmed down enough to explain some of the details. "They had three lateral blow-outs during the trial and they met on Saturday. Dr. Tani has decided to stop the trial. My spy inside of Morikawa said it's like a morgue in the building. Morikawa has been screaming at everyone. PenilePro is dead in Japan." Goro-san started giggling and tried out some of his newly developed English, "You might say they're as limp as a dead tuna."

John was ecstatic. Goro-san's English still needed some work, but he couldn't care less at the moment. John's only regret is that he knew that none of this would ever go public. The entire system would stand shoulder to shoulder to prevent a break in the ranks.

Three hours later John took another call on his intercom. It was Dr. Tani. He wanted to meet John for dinner. He even offered to pay.

John's Lessons

- Translation is as much art as science. Indeed, interpretation is the better word for the process.

- As much as Westerners complain about the vagueness of the

Japanese language, Japanese are very comfortable with it. Vague-ness supports flexibility. Flexibility allows the means to manipulate actions to create results acceptable to the consensus.

- The brake on the entire system is accountability. While the system for clinical trials may seem "rigged," the end results are usually acceptable and even accurate. The fact is that most investigators are caring people who want to do a good job. In the fictitious case of Dr. Tani, who was willing to manufacture a favorable outcome for Morikawa, the trial came to an end when the disparity became *too* great to support *tatemae*. While not transparent, the system works. Most of the time.

- The real danger of the system is that it provides very weak checks and balances on the power broker or powerful person who is motivated by greed and power or unrestricted by conscience. These cases are the exception in Japan, but they are notable because of the inability of the system to deal with such people. Excesses lead to cover-ups and cover-ups in Japan are seldom exposed. Chances are that we will never know the human toll exacted as a result of misconducted clinical trials and defective medical products.

18

John, Dr. Morita, and the Regulatory Application

The dinner with Dr. Tani went very well. He came as close to groveling as a power broker could come. Dr. Tani indicated his enthusiasm for sweeping the entire PenilePro debacle under the nearest rug. But John also made it crystal clear that the price for his scientific rehabilitation was the explicit adherence to the detailed clinical plan put in place by the CRO. It wasn't exactly *dogeza*, the ritual touching of the forehead to *tatami* as an indication of abject apology, but Dr. Tani quietly assented to all of John's demands.

In fact, with Dr. Tani as their new honorary chairman the entire trial seemed to come alive. As John anticipated, the PenilePro mess never went public. But there was no doubt that everyone in Japan's medical and bureaucratic world knew the details and was watching the course of the MTI trial with unabashed interest. For all of his initial draw-backs, Dr. Tani's blessing on the new trial constituted a trial-by-fire for the entire concept. If it worked, there was real hope that change could happen. John knew Japan well enough not to hold any unrealistic hopes for quick change. If it happened, it would be organic and restrained. But now there was hope and even a kind of enthusiasm. Even Dr. Tani caught it.

The trial was building momentum. Every completed case card was one step closer to John's goal and success. After every procedure, John and Dr. Morita personally spoke with each patient and reviewed the case card. The case cards turned out to be the most challenging part of the entire process. In some trials, doctors sat down and filled out all of the detailed data for every patient who had participated during the entire six month trial. John was not yet beyond feeling cynical. They must have wonderful memories to remember patients from six months ago, he thought. But Dr. Ono and his fellow investigators knew that John and Dr. Morita would be there waiting after each procedure. It was enough to force their grudging compliance.

The hard work paid off and MTI finished its trial six months ahead of schedule. It turned out that they had a surfeit of patients and doctors wanting to be enrolled in the study.

Everyone on the MTI team from Dr. Tani on down was convinced of the reliability and persuasiveness of the trial data. But another hurdle remained, maybe the highest hurdle. Good data meant nothing if Koseisho rejected it. This meant that their regulatory submission would have to face the toughest possible scrutiny. Given the stink of the entire Morikawa mess, Koseisho would be under the microscope on this one. There was no way they could slide by.

According to Bruce and Dr. Morita, the only contact they were allowed with Koseisho officials would be during an unofficial administrative guidance session. John and Dr. Morita treated themselves to a taxi on their way to the Ministry. They sat in front of a ministry official who looked no more than twenty-five years old. John's hands trembled as he politely pushed the list of materials they had prepared for this unofficial review across the table to the young man. His name was Kan-san. He studied the list for several minutes. John stared intently at the young fellow, restraining any urge to leap across the table and shake him into compliance. Finally, Kan-san took a breath and rendered his verdict. "Everything seems to be in order."

John let out an audible sigh of relief. Victory might be theirs. "You mean with this data that our application will be approved?"

"*Shuu...*," Kan seemed to have sprung a leak. "You can say that if you want to say so," Kan-san said after some thought.

John turned to Dr. Morita. "What did he say?"

"He said that you can say that if you want to say so."

John stared first at Kan-san, who sat impassive, and then turned back to Dr. Morita. "I know what he said. But what did he mean?"

Dr. Morita glanced away. "I don't know."

The next few minutes were like a scene from Abbott and Costello's "Who's on first?" routine. Dr. Morita kept glancing at John, trying to keep him calm and polite in front of this bureaucratic demigod.

John had had enough of this oblique stuff and his American need to be direct could be ignored no longer. "Mr. Kan, please tell me as directly as possible. What is your opinion of our application?"

Kan smiled and said, "We had a very nice discussion and I think we accomplished a great deal."

John leaned even further over the table, wondering if Kan had a family and if they would miss him after he strangled him to death. John vaguely felt Dr. Morita's restraining hand on his shoulder. John hesitated. Dr. Morita stood up bowed at a forty-five-degree angle and poured out enough *keigo* to indicate that he, John and MTI occupied a space below insects on the evolutionary ladder and Kan-san was up there in the clouds with the gods. John stood up and followed his cue and bowed at a forty-five-degree angle, muttering something about cockroaches. If Kan-san heard him, he failed to let on. He seemed delighted with the meeting, as John and Dr. Morita bowed their way out of the divine presence.

Preparing the actual data submission package was a monumental exercise. Dr. Morita had prepared a list of the requirements for the document. It was not a short list.

1. Translated copy of the operator's manual (106 pages)
2. Translated copy of the FDA 510(k) or PMA application package (563 pages)
3. Translated QC and SOP (84 pages)
4. Translated product specification list complete with diagrams (81 pages)
5. List and description of all components
6. Detailed description of the function of each component
7. Internal and external dimensions
8. Weight of the device and all of its components
9. List of all raw materials used, down to the base compounds
10. List of all safety features
11. Complete description of operating method and training instructions

12. A complete list of cautions for use
13. Complete (sterilization) method and references
14. Methods of testing device integrity
15. Clinical Trial Data
    a) Protocol
    b) All case cards
    c) Informed consent cards
    d) Statistical analysis
    e) Results of the study

Dr. Morita disappeared during the preparation process. It had been a week since John had seen him when they met at 6:00 a.m. on the morning of their application submission. John was shocked at his appearance. John's first thought was that he had died and been reincarnated as a corpse. Dr. Morita was sitting behind a giant stack of paper well over three feet high.

"My God! Is that what we have to submit to Koseisho?" John asked.

Dr. Morita barely nodded, lost in the concentration of threading what looked like a blue shoelace through small holes that had been punched into each sheet with a king-size needle. "*Chikusho,*" he yelped, exclaiming the Japanese form of "shit!" when he stuck his palm with the needle.

John ran off to get a band-aid from the company first-aid kit. When he ran back he saw Dr. Morita staring like a zombie at the document.

"There is blood on the paper!" he muttered, aghast at the prospect of a speck of blood no larger than a pinhead in diameter.

"It's OK," John told him.

"No!" he shouted, ripping the string out of the paper and removing the stained page from the stack.

While printing another page, John asked, "Why not use a binder or a stapler?"

"It is not acceptable," he grunted.

"Why?" John queried.

"I don't know," he replied vacantly. "That's just the way it is."

After checking and rechecking the required three sets of documents expertly strung by the wounded hand of Dr. Morita, they were ready to venture to Koseisho.

"Off to Koseisho we go," John chirped cheerfully, trying to elevate the mood. The sky was dark. It was rainy season and the air hung like a wet washcloth.

"We are not going to Koseisho." John thought he was joking.

"The package must first be reviewed by the local city office for correctness and completeness. Once accepted by them, it will then be forwarded to the Ministry of Health and Welfare. We will not have any direct contact with Koseisho."

"Oh" was about all John could muster. He just didn't have the energy or heart to listen to one of Dr. Morita's "explanations."

It started raining. Morita-san looked approvingly at the scene. "This is good," he said.

"Why?" John asked, not really wanting to know the answer.

"Because we will be wet."

"Oh."

After finding the correct elevators they went to the twenty-eighth floor of the giant government complex located in Shinjuku. Merely going through Shinjuku gave John the shivers. He just hoped that one of his erstwhile homeless buddies wasn't hanging around. But the feeling he got from the government building was even odder. It felt like one of Japan's old feudal castles wrapped in modern garb, with Japan's new bureaucratic samurai moving to and fro in their identical blue-suited garb. Armed with reams of paper, not double swords, these men appeared even more dangerous. These men would not cut him down on the street, but they could cut down MTI's regulatory application. Stepping out of the elevator, Morita-san looked approvingly at their wet suits and disheveled hair. Outside the bureau door stood several men in similar attire, smoking cigarettes and pacing back and forth as if awaiting the arrival of a child. They, too, had their own stacks of paper carefully strung with the proper string. John was amused to see that one of the men had a bandage on his palm. He smiled knowingly at this probable puncture wound.

While he could tell that Dr. Morita and the others knew each other, no one spoke. Like rival sport teams, the regulatory staff of one team apparently did not mingle with another. When absolutely necessary, interchanges were made in hushed tones and with a false smile. At precisely 9:01 a.m., the steel gray doors swung open. There stood the mighty bureaucrat. Cheap suit. Sandals. The knowing postural slouch of someone accustomed to twelve-hour days of laconically pushing paper from one stack to the next. In unison, all the men intoned a respectful *"Ohayo gozaimasu"* to the bureaucrat as they stepped into his domain.

There was a small vestibule for guests. The government had graciously set aside working tables complete with paper cutters and, of course, strings. Behind the vestibule was an ocean of desks manned by the best and brightest of Japan's universities, all diligently at work. MTI was second in line. John's arms ached with the weight of the paper. A puddle had formed below him and began to contribute to the puddles of the person directly in front and behind.

Finally, it was their turn and they respectfully handed their stack to a well-groomed man in his late twenties. He immediately and expertly riffled through the stack. His hands were lightening quick. Page after page shot momentarily in front of his eye for review. He occasionally made comments John could not comprehend. Each comments was associated with a small piece of paper inserted into the stack. After standing at attention for about forty minutes, John's feet and shoulders beginning to throb. They said *"Hai!"* more times than John could count. Just when John thought he was going to faint, the ordeal was over. The young bureaucrat samurai, their gateway to Koseisho, smiled and handed the stack back to Dr. Morita.

Dr. Morita bowed deeply and thanked the young man profusely. They dragged the stack over to the working table and Dr. Morita deftly pulled out the string and began reviewing the notes scribbled on the little pieces of paper. After an hour and a half they were racing to make the necessary changes. It was an odd scene. There was an entire group of men trying not to sweat, trying not to looked stressed, with their hearts pounding as they worked side-by-side to meet the detailed instructions of their overlord. Finally, they had gone through the entire document and returned to the line. It was even heavier this time.

After some obligatory pleasantries, the nice young man remarked approvingly that they seemed to be working very diligently and seemed to approve of moist, rumpled suits and stressed faces. They had suffered appropriately. Once again he riffled expertly through their document, which looked so perfect early in the morning. It now looked shopworn and less than compelling. Pages were uneven, torn. John also noticed with total dismay that more of those damned little white pieces of paper were being inserted into their document. Each page examined, comments made. They returned to their working table. Dr. Morita seemed unfazed by it all, but John felt like screaming.

Most of the day was gone. They had a great deal of work before they could approach their master with a revised application. They returned to MTI office with a mound of torn and marked paper in the trunk of the car. It was raining.

It took them four full days of work to revise the document and more than a month at the city application center to get their application "accepted" by the almighty samurai bureaucrat. They made countless, mostly meaningless, changes to the document. Again, they stood before their young master who riffled once more through the document. He stopped at one page, picked up a pen to write on one of those damned little pieces of white paper and was about to insert it when he looked at their faces and invisibly made the judgment that they had suffered enough. They had paid their dues. He picked up a long-handled *inkan*, or stamp, and very expertly stamped the three copies of their document. Their application was now accepted. It was now in the hands of invisible bureaucrats at Koseisho. Learning the game, John maintained his composure as they bowed repeatedly and expressed their inexpressible thanks.

John's Lessons

- There is an almost mystical quality to the power of Japan's ministries. One can feel this power in the form of unspoken guidelines that motivate regulatory executives to engage in odd behavior such as: filing applications when it is raining to look humble and downtrodden; appearing at the office before opening time to show sincerity; and using traditional binding methods such as string for documents.

- The irony is that we believe these strictures are more powerful among the governed than they are in the minds of the government officials themselves. But the lack of transparency and vagueness of the system creates a pervasive sense of being "safe not sorry." Culturally, Japanese are conditioned to look at the bureaucracy in terms of profound power, even life or death. This deeply inculcated sense of deference hardly encourages Japanese to push back.

- In our experience, regulatory submissions are rejected on the first or second time simply as a "matter of course." It may be a simple process of one-upmanship. Again, it is simply better to play the game according to the unwritten rules. Losers have no recourse.

- Everyone in the regulatory business has heard stories of bureaucrats being downright nasty. Our experience has been quite to the contrary. The front line officials tend to be very reasonable, pleasant and seemingly helpful to their regulatory counterpart. That is, as long as everyone stays within the rules of the game.

- The application process for medical regulatory approvals is quite convoluted. Upon submission, no further discussions with Koseisho are permitted. The actual submission is through the local ward or city office. In most large wards, this is through an office dedicated to this purpose. The receipt of the final approval or rejection is also through the local office. The reason for such a system was to insulate the MHW from unwanted direct influence or lobbying from applicants.

- Once the application package is accepted, it moves to the MHW. At this point, the MHW passes it on to researchers, usually academic, for review. This person may be the president of the appropriate *gakkai,* but is almost certain to be a power broker or elderly statesman. In the case of new medical technologies, a panel hearing may be held but there will be little substantive discussion at the hearing. The real debate is held before the panel hearing and will be the decision of the power broker.

- There are also cases when the power broker throws the application back to the manufacturer after the first round for clarification or additional data. After this exercise is complete, the power broker will then approve the application. It will then be reviewed by Ministry officials, who will forward it to the ward office, who will send a notification post card. When picking up the approval, tradition dictates that you should not ask questions. Just grab the approval, bow, and run!

19

John and the Reality of Medical Reimbursement

The sense of exhilaration and relief that came with the acceptance of their regulatory application was short-lived. Very short-lived.

Seated at the MTI conference table across from John and Dr. Morita, Bruce set off the reimbursement depth charge.

John sat there in shock. "What do you mean that we will fall under the same reimbursement as a run-of-the-mill penile implant? Our *hoken tensu* (insurance reimbursement points) should be at least double. MTI's products are vastly superior. What about the pre-set erector settings? Or the diagnostic capabilities? Why did we even bother with the entire application process if that's the case. We'll never recover our investment at the current reimbursement."

"Calm down," Bruce replied soothingly. "This is very complicated, so just cool your jets for a few minutes and listen." John nodded and took a deep breath. Bruce continued. "A product is approved either as a 'me-too' or as a new device. Typically, a me-too device is inserted within the established category of reimbursement. Thus it would be billable in June. But, the MTI product is a brand new technology application. There has never been a penile implant which can screen for cervical cancer and detect STDs. So, we need to apply for reimbursement separately."

John shrugged his shoulders. "Sounds great. Let's do it."

"Well, it's not quite that simple. A penile implant falls under the medical device rules, and diagnostic portion under the Japanese Pharmaceutical Affairs Law covering *in vitro* diagnostics."

John couldn't resist an interjection. "But it's an *in vivo* device."

Bruce dismissed John's comment with a wave of his hand. "Regardless, we need to get the penile implant portion reimbursed as a device. This reimbursement will be at me-too levels, the same as your other non-enhanced products. In addition, the diagnostic portion cannot be reimbursed to physicians or users at one time. Instead, the reimbursement has to be based on each diagnostic result. Are you following me?"

"I think so," John replied tentatively. "If what I think you're about to tell me is true, I think I'm going to be very excited."

Bruce started chuckling. "Prepare to be very excited. If we can document and submit each result to the patient's physician, the physician can apply for reimbursement each time the patient uses the device for its diagnostic purpose."

John could barely contain himself and started bouncing up and down in his chair. "You mean, we can apply for reimbursement every time a patient has sex?"

Bruce smiled back but held back from bouncing up and down. "Yep. Of course, the patient has to remember to print out a result."

"I can't wait to tell Big Ed about this. He'll go bananas."

"Don't count your chickens yet," Bruce cautioned. "But if we can swing this, MTI will be absolutely golden. Doctors will throw an implant at every male over the age of fifty with a bladder infection. Think of the repeat business! And if MTI could rent the device rather than sell it, you could get a cut of the action every time one of your clients has sex."

John couldn't resist. "I wonder if there's a diagnostic application for palm blisters."

They both roared with laughter. Dr. Morita stared uncomprehendingly at the two crazy foreigners.

John's Lessons

- Of course, the above discussion on reimbursement was done in jest. But many of the messages in it are vital about doing business in Japan, especially if the business involves products that fall under the category of a novel new device. Reimbursement permits physicians and patients the use of the products. Without a good reimbursement level, the incentive to use even good products is reduced. Providing a complete set of rules and details of the reimbursement system is beyond the scope of this book, but the following points are important to keep firmly in mind.

- The level of reimbursement and the frequency at which reimbursement may be charged to a particular patient's account will dictate to a great extent the commercial success of the product. The MHW knows this and they use it repeatedly to their advantage to manipulate the practice of medicine.

- Reimbursement rates are jointly established by four groups: 1) the government ministry, Chuikyo; 2) professional groups, usually *gakkai* heads; 3) industry groups; and 4) the Social Insurance Agency. Of these groups, industry seems to have the least power. Upon closer examination, however, we find that industry is also the only group with private money. Industry engages in an extensive *tatemae* effort to demonstrate cost-effectiveness, general efficacy, and the overall positive effect of its products on the Japanese health care system. The more important task is to influence other members of the group.

  This influence occurs at several levels: 1) The power brokers in the medical professional group can be influenced by discussion, debate or, sometimes, the old fashioned way—graft. 2) While the two governmental bodies have been caught in blatant cases of graft, the more subtle and traditional method is to employ strategic government employees after retirement. This practice is referred to as *amakudari*, or "god descending from heaven." This is an open practice, tolerated in the spirit of government-industry cooperation. The practice of *amakudari* has been criticized in recent years and there is discussion about ending the practice.

- Reimbursement is readjusted every two years. The system in general is designed to reward new and innovative technology. Older and less useful products tend to get caught on a downward escalator of reimbursement levels.

- The best advice we can give to the ethical business manager in Japan is to: 1) Put reimbursement strategy and tactics at the very top of your list of things to do in planning all aspects of your business. 2) Do not trust a lower-level employee to simply take care of the reimbursement issue. Keep informed and participate in each stage of the process. 3) If you do not receive adequate reimbursement, don't sell it in Japan and publicize the fact that the Japanese public is being denied access to a wonderful product. That is one way to get the attention of the bureaucracy.

20

John Does Distribution—and Fails

John had been in Japan for nearly three years. As he reviewed those turbulent years, John recognized that he had made just about every mistake possible. But he had survived. MTI was doing well if not exactly thriving in the way he had hoped. He had been saved by people like Bruce, Dr. Morita, and even Goro-san. He had had his share of good and bad luck. But now it was time to take the next step and consider how to really grow the business.

With reimbursement and regulatory approval behind them, the next big hurdle was distribution. This was the toughest nut to crack. Medical product distribution in Japan may be one of the world's most arcane puzzles, John thought, as he started to put together his plan of action. John did his homework and studied his options. One thing he had learned over and over in Japan the hard way was that careful preparation was the key to success.

His homework had yielded the following points:

1) There are no national medical distributors in Japan. Some claim to be national, but typically they are part of a loose affiliation of distributors that may cover much of the country. Traditionally, medical distributors in Japan have strong geographic limitations and little access to other areas.

2) There are over over five thousand medical distributors in Japan. They range in size from giants to one-man operations. Besides

their geographical limitations, distributors are limited by their human relations with accounts. Sometimes a manufacturer will have to use two distributors for hospitals located across the street from each other.

3) Medical distributors exercise considerable leverage over the hospitals and clinics they serve. This leverage begins with the human element and extends to the generous payment terms of net 180 days and even net 360 days that they sometimes offer to their customers. Terminating a relationship can be a financially painful process for the hospital and its doctors.

4) Medical distributors in Japan are now under tremendous pressure and their numbers have shrunk by an estimated twenty percent in the last five years. Reasons for the shrinkage include the generational turnover at small family-owned distributors, more conservative lending practices at banks, and squeezed margins. Hospitals are also feeling the pinch and have scissored the distributors with their own requests for better terms. Everyone in the industry expects bankruptcies and consolidation to accelerate.

5) Koseisho has developed a sophisticated method of manipulating distributors to meet structural needs. This system includes: a) obtaining accurate pricing data from distributors for the biannual pricing review; and b) passing legislation which bars manufacturers from setting end-user pricing. Intended to spur competition at the customer level, there is in fact continued "informal" guidance by manufacturers. Because hospitals seldom open new accounts for new distributors, the failure to adhere to the informal guidance provides an opportunity for profiteering by the distributor.

John's grand strategy culminated with his introduction to a Mr. Sakamoto, president of one Japan's larger medical distribution companies. John rubbed his hands together while waiting for Sakamoto-san to return from the rest room. They were seated in, of all places, the dark confines of the Passion Fruit Club, where John first set off on his ill-fated romance with the now long-gone Hitomi. The place was suggested by Sakamoto and John was willing to test the waters again, hoping that all the ghosts had been exorcised.

Dinner had been at an exclusive sushi restaurant near the LDP (Liberal Democratic Party) headquarters in Miyakezaka. Everyone was fairly well lubricated as they watched Kumi and Yumi giggling as they performed their duo magic trick with match sticks. John was numb with boredom but understood the game well enough to clap his hands in feigned delight as they completed the grand finale. Sakamoto's lieutenants, Shimbo and Nagata, ignored the hand show, preferring to fondle the young ladies thighs before their hands got slapped away at the conclusion of the show.

This was already John's third meeting with the distributor. The first two meetings had not gone particularly well, but John was hopeful that they were just warm-ups for the big show tonight when they got down to real business. Sakamoto Shoji was a large distributor with excellent access to urology centers in many of the large hospitals of the Kanto region. It was a perfect fit for both MTI and Sakamoto Shoji.

The white-haired president returned and was rewarded with a hot *oshibori* towel by the cute Kumi. Or maybe it Yumi, John couldn't be sure. He plopped his somewhat oversized rear end onto the low couch next to John with the requisite exhalation and touched John lightly on his knee. John knew this as a sign it was time to talk business. In his vastly improved Japanese, John said "Perhaps we should talk some business."

The effect was immediate. The two lieutenants stopped their fondling and one even straightened his tie. The girls immediately stopped their off-color banter and put away the match sticks. Even Sakamoto sat more erect and leaned forward toward John. It was time to talk turkey.

The initial discussions went well. Sakamoto obviously wanted the MTI product line. But things went downhill as the details emerged, particularly when John mentioned the intended area of coverage.

"What do you mean, we can only distribute in the Kanto area!" Sakamoto retorted in abrupt Japanese. "We are a national distributor. And what is this list of 640 hospitals and clinics in the Kanto area that we would be excluded from? I don't understand this at all."

"Sakamoto-san," John said with as much respect as he could muster. "Those are the hospitals and clinics that you do not have an account with. And, we are aware of your national distribution capabilities, but we most respectfully wish to offer you the products in your strongest area, which, I believe, is the capital area."

Sakamoto pulled back, looked at John for a moment and then motioned for his lieutenants to huddle. While they spoke in hushed tones, John glanced at the neighboring table noticing that Yumi and Kumi were performing the same match-stick trick with a group of drunk *sararimen* trying to fondle them. John sighed, wondering how an American boy from Utah ended up doing this kind of thing for a living.

Finally, Sakamoto broke his reverie. "I don't know where you got this list. But even if the list may be partially correct, we have ways into all of these accounts." Sakamoto drew himself as fully erect as his gut would allow. The lieutenants did their best imitation of their boss. Sakamoto continued. "As for our distribution capabilities outside of the Kanto, well, we are as good as anyone."

John knew he had hit a brick wall on this one. He decided to take another tack. "OK, we'll discuss territories later. I will certainly consider expanding the territory if you can demonstrate your capabilities. But please understand that MTI has strict rules about this policy." John long ago had learned the effective Japanese negotiating tactic of turning aside issues by blaming non-present authority.

They continued the discussion for several hours more, basically covering the same ground over and over again. Endurance was key, John knew. He also knew from his extensive homework that giving Sakamoto the distribution rights outside of the Kanto would condemn MTI products to at least a three and possibly a four layer distribution network. That would blast the end-user price right through the ceiling and hinder his goal of capturing maximum market share quickly. The reality, as John knew only too well, was that the number of hospitals and clinics in the Kanto (region) not covered by Sakamoto was actually closer to one-thousand. But he had chosen to save the president's face.

Nothing was decided that night, but John promised to fax Sakamoto a copy of MTI's standard distribution agreement in the morning.

It took just about an hour for the shit to hit the fan after faxing the standard agreement to Sakamoto Shoji. At 10:05 John took a call from one of Sakamoto's lieutenants, the one who had been fondling Yumi's right thigh, or maybe it was Kumi's left thigh. Anyway, the lieutenant breathlessly spoke with John. "The president has many questions about the contract. He would like to meet with you by all means today."

He waited as John perused his appointment book, which happened to be full of meetings with other distributors. John decided this was more important and canceled those meetings in preparation for a meeting at Sakamoto Shoji at 3:00 p.m.

John never ceased to be amazed by the austere atmosphere and clutter of the offices of a Japanese distributor. Paper was stacked everywhere. Each desk groaned under its fair share of paper. Even the floors had been assigned filing duties. The walls were dingy, with vintage sixties dark wood paneling holding the collective energy of sixty people who seemed to be racing back and forth on matters of earthshaking importance. But what totally amazed John on any visit was the computer count. Sixty people and there were only two computers and these looked to be old-fashioned *wapro*, or Japanese word processors. Given that surprising fact, John thought, maybe it wasn't so unusual that half the desks in the room appeared to support an abacus.

John was led into Sakamoto's equally unpretentious office by a middle aged OL in a blue suit and slippers. Sakamoto was seated in a chair, flanked by his two lieutenants and a new person. After the perfunctory exchange of pleasantries and a slurp or two of tea, Sakamoto made the introduction. "This is Kawachi, our regulatory affairs director. He is a licensed pharmacist." He looked nervous, John thought, maybe like John would try to mug him. John vowed to himself to resort to violence only in the last resort.

Sakamoto-san continued. "John-san, we know that you are relatively new to Japan. So, I have asked Kawachi here to help explain the complexities of Japan's regulatory system to you. After reviewing your contract draft, it appears that a few items need to be revised." Kawachi began fidgeting very, very nervously in his chair.

"Which part of the agreement is a problem?" John asked innocently, knowing exactly what was going to happen next.

Kawachi began mumbling, attempting to educate John. "MTI cannot hold the *shonin*. Only an authorized importer, like Sakamoto Shoji, can hold the *shonin* and import products." Kawachi looked relieved, happy to still be alive.

John feigned puzzlement. He opened his briefcase, extracting a copy of the approval documents that MTI had finally received a few weeks before. "But, we do hold a *shonin*, through an in-country caretaker."

Kawachi took the documents and after a few moments, began to sweat. He wondered if foreigners really did shoot people for no reason at all.

He forced out a few words. "I don't understand how this is possible." He shuddered, glancing at his company's president. Either way he looked, this guy was in trouble.

John held up his hand to prevent further carnage and explained. "It's no wonder that you have not heard of this, since the rules are quite new." John thought, "Yeah, real new. Since 1984." He continued to explain to his dismayed audience about the rules of in-country caretakers. By the time he finished Kawachi was slumped down and Sakamoto looked very concerned.

In a shallow voice, the president asked, "You mean you could switch your distributor any time you want?"

"Of course, we would never do such a thing," John added quickly.

The room was locked in silence. Finally, Sakamoto solemnly pronounced, "We will need to study this situation further."

John waited a week, but never heard again from anyone at Sakamoto Shoji. John's gambit had failed.

Bruce, Goro and Dr. Morita sat around the conference table, taking turns raking John over the coals for his ill-advised struggle with Sakamoto Shoji.

"You prepared too well," admonished Dr. Morita.

John was stunned. "What do you mean, I prepared too well?"

Bruce stepped in. "I think what Dr. Morita means is that while you need to prepare well, you can't rub their noses in it. You embarrassed them and left them with nowhere to go. Worst of all, you caused Sakamoto to lose face in front of his people. On a scale of one to ten, that rates a negative number."

Even Goro got his licks in. "Your goose is heated."

Where did Goro come up with this stuff, John wondered. "You mean, my goose is cooked."

Everyone nodded in unison, agreeing on the fate of John's goose.

John tried again to defend his course of action. "Bruce, I did what you told me to do long ago. I took all the cards into my hand. I had the market knowledge card, the regulatory card. I even had the grassroots scientific community card. The only card I dealt them was the product distribution card. What's wrong with that?" John ended, his voice raising plaintively.

"But, you played it wrong, didn't you. John, get your head out of your ass."

"At least, I scared the hell of out 'em, didn't I?"

Goro started giggling. It was contagious. Within seconds, the three of them were laughing uncontrollably. John looked at them helplessly, resenting that he was the butt of some joke they understood and he didn't. Finally, Goro stopped long enough to say, "Do you actually think that Sakamoto Shoji, with over four-hundred million dollars in annual turnover and four-hundred MRs in the field, was quaking in their shoes because of you?"

John turned red. "Boots," he said. Laughter swept the table again.

Frustrated, angry and tired of beating his head against this unyielding wall, John stood to escape. "The hell with Japan and to hell with you guys."

"Sit down," Bruce requested.

Grudgingly, John obeyed.

Miss Hirata arrived and served them coffee and they continued with the post-mortem.

Bruce led off. "As Dr. Morita said, your first mistake was to show them how strong your hand was. Domestically, Japanese distributors are used to holding all the cards. For every John and MTI who pays their dues, there are a hundred Western medical companies who repeat the mistakes over and over again and never learn. The liberalization of regulations that MTI has benefited from are relatively recent and the bottom line is that most companies just don't move up the learning curve. Sakmoto's shock at confronting a foreigner who understands the game is understandable; he's probably never seen one before. Most foreign executives who land at Narita couldn't find their ass if they were sitting on their hands."

John only needed to think back on his own experience before to understand the truth of Bruce's words.

Dr. Morita cut in. "But it sounds like you're holding the *shonin* was the last straw."

"Of course." Goro interjected. "In my Morikawa days, we didn't even care what was in the contract. If we owned the *shonin*, we owned the business and there was nothing the foreign company could do about it. I remember Morikawa himself laughing, privately of course, at our partners when the realization of their predicament showed on their faces. Morikawa especially loved to see a hotshot American captain of industry eat humble cake rather than have zero sales for one or two years."

John nodded approvingly. Goro had come a long way. "But what's the point of the entire exercise if no one will do business with you?"

"John," Bruce said in that patronizing tone of voice that John simply hated. "It's all a matter of finesse. It takes time to build relationships and you have to take what your partner gives you. You needed to position the regulatory card in a positive way—that you were saving them years of work and hundreds of thousands of dollars. They have an immediate product for distribution. That's worth gold in Japan's medical world today. If they wanted the *shonin*, and you really felt that they were the people you wanted to work with, you should have said OK. After all, you control the flow of product, and if you have your own parallel *shonin*, you're covered. You hold the card, but let them hold their own card. As the house, you win in the event of a tie."

Goro couldn't resist another chance to gently chide his boss. "But the biggest mistake you made was to think you scared Sakamoto. No matter how many cards you hold, distributors still have a great deal of power here. They control the contracts with the end-users and they spend a lot on developing and keeping those relationships. They can be valuable allies if used properly."

"That's right," Bruce inserted, "A good distributor deserves your respect. They've worked hard to survive. But the biggest reason he was not afraid of you is that he knew you could never succeed. And the way you set out to do it, there is no question you would have failed."

That last statement shocked John. He realized he was guilty of numerous tactical errors, but he thought his strategy had been sound. Obviously, he was wrong, John thought ruefully.

"Your plan was a good one. In fact, you did everything right. Where you screwed up was the scale of your operation. From what you told us, you were going to set up some twenty or thirty distribution contracts throughout Japan. We both know that is the minimum you will need to provide one to two tier coverage to most users. But, how were you going to manage those contracts? Most big companies have dozens of dealer representatives. Some companies treat dealers better than they do their customers! Even if you were able get everyone to sign the contract, you cold have never have managed them effectively. Internal squabbles among dealers, pricing, marketing. It would have been unmanageable."

"My plan was to increase staff as revenues grew." John tried meekly to defend his grand strategy.

"OK, let's say you pull the rabbit out of the hat and get through that phase. Did you really think that you could have twenty-five companies importing directly?" Bruce looked pointedly at John.

"That was the general idea," John said.

"Think about it. That would be virtually impossible. Remember, you are the in-country caretaker. You also have the responsibility to inform each end-user of problems which could affect patient care. You also must inform both Koseisho and the home office if similar problems are found in Japan. It is theoretically possible, but given the staffing and management, hardly practical. Besides, it would drive Koseisho crazy to manage all of the paperwork. Believe me, they'd find a way to get you back into line."

John felt like a human punching bag, with uppercuts followed by jab after jab. "If that's the case, I have to ask again, why did we go through this entire process?"

"It's all part of the process. You simply took the first step," Goro said kindly. "Don't you see? MTI can't simply step in and make all the rules in Japan. Even a multinational has to settle for less than the best when they are setting up their business here. The good news is that MTI is finally a player in the game. We hold some very good cards and the other players are willing to let us play. The only card left for us to get is the patient card. With another few years of hard work and good products, we'll be at the top of the heap."

"What does this mean in practical terms?" John asked the trio.

All three started talking at once, but Dr. Morita and Goro let Bruce articulate their common concerns. "John, first you should have explored you options. For a company your size, working with a manufacturer of similar products, may be the way to go. While their distribution system may be flabby, it is probably managed well. Of course, you may have to give up some of your name recognition, which can be a difficult barrier to overcome later."

"If a manufacturer is not available, a distributor, or even a *shosha*, may be in order, with all the usual caveats to think about. But, until you are ready to start importing yourself, you need to limit the lines of import. Once you reach critical mass, you can take over the import function. You already have the *shonin*, and it is something you should be able to build into any distribution contract. When exclusive contracts expire, renegotiate non-exclusive contracts or limit the territory. In the end, you will end up where you want to be, but it may take a several years to get there." Bruce sat back.

Goro, waiting for his chance to speak, said, "The key is to be here, stay close to the market, and take control of the process."

21

John Takes Control

John was still in the same suit from the previous day when he returned to his office at 9:00 a.m. Miss Bamba was horrified to see him, seemingly reverted to his past bad habits. John was going to miss her when she got married next month and left her job for the honorable role of wife to a *sarariman*. But finding a replacement for the Bamba was the least of John's problems.

He had spent much of the night wandering around Tokyo, finally ending up at his old haunt, the Royal Kanda Capsule Hotel. He needed time and the right place to think and somehow he wound up in front of his old buddy at the front desk. By morning he had reached resolution on his dilemma. The criticism from the previous day still stung and he hated the idea that he had quickly bowed to Bruce's and the others' ideas. He wanted to make his own way through this. But he had to admit that every time he did something completely on his own, he screwed it up big time. Recalling their laughter the previous day made the pill all the more bitter to swallow.

John resolved to do it his way, but use the resources he had at hand. He asked Miss Bamba to call the group together immediately for a command performance, no excuses accepted. An hour later they walked into the MTI conference room. Seeing John in his rumpled suit and bloodshot eyes, Bruce was about to make one of his smart-ass comments. But he stopped short at John's stern visage and outstretched palm. They sat down, waiting for John's message of obvious importance.

"Gentlemen, we are going to find a partner for MTI in Japan and we are going to do it right. Bruce, I want a list of the top ten manufacturers that match these basic criteria." John's tone allowed no room for dissent. He walked to the white board and wrote the following:

1) National distribution coverage
2) Deep pockets
3) No competitive threat potential

"Yes, sir!" Bruce sat erect and saluted. He sensed an entirely new dynamic at work here, but wasn't exactly sure what it was yet.

John continued. "I want everything you can find out about them. I want to know what sports the president likes and who in the organization would be responsible for making decisions. I also want to see a history of their other relationships with foreign companies. Lastly, I want you to propose an initial entry point and the best person to use as our *nakodo*, or go-between."

Bruce's smirk vanished. He sat in shock. Their roles seemed reversed and he didn't particularly like it. "OK," he barely managed.

"How long will it take?" John asked.

"Boy, this will take a couple of months," he replied.

"You've got a month." John snapped back.

"Hey," Bruce said, beginning to rise.

"And I'll pay double your normal fee." Bruce hesitated and then fell back into the chair. "OK."

John was rolling now. He looked at his next victim. "Dr. Morita," he nearly shouted. Dr. Morita shot to attention and responded with a *"Hai,"* much the way he responded to his respected *kendo* teacher long ago.

"I want you to make sure that all of the approvals are ready to be transferred. I want a copy of the approvals bound into a hard-cover book and embossed with the MTI company logo. Hell, with as much money as we have invested in these things they are worth more than their weight in gold, they may as well look like it." John was glaring at him.

Dr. Morita had never heard of such a thing, but nodded uncomfortably in agreement.

Next target. "Goro. I want you to put together a multimedia presentation in both English and Japanese. We'll use the numbers generated by Bruce to demonstrate our clear value in the Japanese market and the strengths of MTI's technology. The goal is to have anyone who sees it to want to hand us his wallet and commit a ton of money and resources to the distribution of our products."

The three men sat in shocked silence. John refused to let go of the group. "While you are working on your projects, I will work on a written prospectus to accompany Goro-san's presentation. Goro-san, I will need this translated and done well. We need to find someone that can turn it into a piece of literature." Finally, John stopped talking.

"Where will you get all this money?" was the only thing Goro could say, thinking of the thousands the translation alone would cost.

"You let me worry about that." And John turned on his heel and left the room, leaving his three supporters to stare open-mouthed at the door. Nothing was said, but they all knew that the rules of the game had changed.

Despite his dramatic show of confidence and resolution, John felt only anxiety as he contemplated his choice of action. He thought it important to avoid the gang lest he display a crack in his armor. Only a few steps from his office was a very old temple, with a long flight of stone steps leading up to an oasis of tranquillity in Tokyo's frenetic swirl. John often visited this place, almost thinking of it as his own private property. It was a beautiful early autumn day with bright blue skies and a promise of warmth in the air. He hoped to God that he was doing the right thing. But his plan was simple and good, he thought.

The key was that he had to take control. He could listen to people and benefit from their wisdom, but then he had to make focused plans and follow them through to completion. He remembered the words of his business professor at the University of Washington, Dr. Jay Johnston. Over and over he repeated that the key to business success was commitment, continuity, and focus. John also remembered the professor's other commandment to always keep an eye on the cash. Well, John was certainly screwing that up right now.

His plan was to narrow down the choice of potential partners to two or three and build the approach as a sales scenario. It was crucial to demonstrate the value of the market to the potential partners and then position the regulatory approvals as a contribution by MTI to the relationship, unlike his disastrous lunge at Sakamoto Shoji.

Lastly, he needed to keep the money on the table. John hoped for at least five to ten million dollars from the deal. But it was going to be tricky. Partly because Japanese are great at moving money off the table and partly because he wanted to keep the money in Japan for growing MTI-Japan. He didn't want it repatriated to the MTI in Los Angeles where Big Ed would squander it on some stupid project. That money would be the fuel to send his rocket ship to the moon. With it, he could build the infrastructure that MTI-Japan needed to be truly successful.

John's Lessons

- To get the best results in finding a Japanese partner, you need to first narrow the field by using a specific set of criteria. Never simply hit the streets and approach anyone who will talk to you.

- Partnering should be treated as a sales scenario. A company needs to develop a marketing plan and package to clearly demonstrate the real value to the potential Japanese partner. One of the most important aspects is to know the value of the market and clearly demonstrate the financial potential of the product.

- Any deal which does not include a cash payment is not recommended. A cash payment demonstrates true commitment by the partner.

- Never assume that the Japanese partner can do it all unassisted. The smart player needs clear plans to actively support the partner to help them gain the true value from their investment. Also, in actively supporting a partner, a company needs to remain connected to the market and to the end user, which could be extremely valuable in the future. Active involvement also keeps the partner on notice that they are being watched and are accountable.

22

John Does His Homework

The fruit of Bruce's work was neatly bound in a report sitting on John's desk. He read the material with satisfaction, pleased with the thoroughness. Bruce had identified three potential partners for MTI. One was a large pharmaceutical company, one was a medical device manufacturer of artificial joints and one was a condom manufacturer. The first two made immediate sense to John, but why the condom manufacturer? Wouldn't the distribution routes for a device be completely different?

Bruce carefully explained the criteria assessment in the report during his presentation. "Please remember, the goal wasn't to find the perfect partner, but the best possible partner for MTI in Japan. In the end, there is always a wart or two. Chemistry is also another intangible, but nevertheless crucial ingredient in the mix."

"Let's look at the condom manufacturer. You're right about their distribution strength. But they have some powerful assets in other areas. First, they have a good understanding of the penile market itself." Goro began giggling, drawing a sharp glance from John.

"Second, they have lots of money and they are desperately looking to diversify into new areas. The word on the street is that they're hungry to invest. Third, they do a considerable amount of business with MTI right now."

"What?" John shot upright in his chair.

"This condom company, Shin-Hifu K.K., is the Original Equipment

Manufacturer (OEM) source for much of MTI's latex and rubber components. The erector struts and even the silicon external molds are sourced from Shin-Hifu, among others. This relationship goes back over ten years. If Japan sunk tomorrow, MTI would be underwater for years. The reason you don't know about this is that MTI sources through Shin-Hifu's U.S. dealer.

"I had no idea," John said slowly shaking his head.

"It's not only MTI. Virtually every high-tech product in the world can trace some component or manufacturing process back to Japan. Without Japan, the world's high-tech industries would shut down," Goro contributed with more than just a little pride in his voice.

The MTI Japan team moved ahead quickly, with a powerful new camaraderie based on John's vision. Goro's multimedia presentation was completed. Using PowerPoint, Goro imported photographs, charts and even some real-time video. It looked sharp and made a powerful statement about MTI's potential contribution to a partner's bottom line. One of their ironic discoveries was that Morikawa had unwittingly made their point through its high-price strategy for MTI's products. Now, the Japan market was already conditioned to think of MTI as the Rolls-Royce of penile implants. The key would be to maintain the quality image while building market share.

John's prospectus also neared completion. It was scheduled to go to the printer for the final full-color printing the next day and binding the next week. The only hitch was on Dr. Morita's end. His first attempt to produce a regulatory package was something like a cardboard box with the traditional Japanese binding strings. John sent him back to the drawing board. The second attempt was bound as John requested, but Dr. Morita insisted on poking three neatly spaced holes and tying the strings tightly around the spine of the document. Old habits die hard. On his third attempt, Dr. Morita finally produced a document without strings, one that looked as valuable as the contents. John was delighted with the final product, but Dr. Morita continued to look at the stringless document with discomfort. No strings left untied was Dr. Morita's regulatory motto.

John's original timeline was to conclude a deal within three to four months of identifying their short list of three potential partners. They missed their window, but it was not for lack of hard work and diligence. No one could have predicted the events that transpired.

It was six months since their first meeting with Shin-Hifu K.K. The MTI team had had numerous meetings with the other two partners, long meetings extending from the chairmen of both companies down to the section-chief level, the operational executives that would make the business sink or swim. Nothing seemed to click with either company. Either there were structural issues or the chemistry was off. The negotiations didn't stop, but they didn't seem to be moving ahead either. John was tempted to tell both "thanks, but no thanks."

Bruce strongly cautioned him to keep them on the line. Although Shin-Hifu was their preferred partner, they needed to play the game out to the end. "You never want to let a company feel too comfortable during the negotiations. If they think they are the only game in town, you lose all of your negotiating power. You have to make them pay for the right to have exclusive negotiations. You also have to set a deadline, or things could drag on for years!" Bruce repeated over and over again.

The negotiations began smoothly. It was obvious that both sides badly wanted a deal to happen. There were long business discussions during the day followed by long nighttime sessions lubricated by copious amounts of alcohol. MTI's earlier decision to hire an honorary chairman, Dr. Murakami, also reaped huge dividends as Dr. Murakami happened to be a golfing buddy with the vice-chairman of Shin-Hifu K.K. Their deal had been blessed at the very top.

One thing odd about the negotiations was the extent to which Shin-Hifu relied upon MTI for an understanding about the penile implant market in Japan. After years of hard work, John and his MTI team knew as much about the market and its intricacies as anyone in the business. The Shin-Hifu negotiating team hungrily absorbed all of MTI's data on pricing, insurance reimbursement and competitive activities. Their due diligence went beyond the pale, though. They double and triple-checked every detail. In the end, they complimented John and his team for being almost Japanese in his mastery of the details. It was a moment of great pride to John.

Perhaps the most powerful weapon in MTI's arsenal was their

grassroots level of support in the academic community. Repentant and reformed, Dr. Tani led the charge on their behalf. His support was unwavering. His position as head of the Penile Implant Association and MTI's honorary chairman of clinical testing left little wiggle room for the Shin-Hifu team to maneuver. The market was loud and clear: MTI's products were valuable and first-rate.

In America, this combination of factors would have led to slam-dunk deal concluded in a few weeks. But this was Japan, and John learned that nothing is ever a slam-dunk here.

At the first meeting with each potential partner, John presented a list of three absolutely non-negotiable points:

1) The Japanese partner would be required to make a signifi-
   - cant up-front monetary commitment to MTI;
2) MTI would have ongoing access to all regulatory approvals; and
3) The Japanese partner would have to adopt a market-share strategy.

Each and every meeting began with Shin-Hifu's team detailing why an up-front monetary commitment was difficult, why it was technically difficult not to hold the *shonin* themselves and why a market share strategy was very difficult in Japan. John knew the speech by heart after the tenth time. Bruce was the most agitated, growing odder and odder with each repetition.

At each meeting, the MTI team would repeat in equally excruciating detail why these three absolutes were non-negotiable. If Shin-Hifu was truly unable to meet the three conditions, perhaps it would be better to discontinue discussions and not waste each other's time. The marathon meetings continued. They met a dozen times over the next four months.

It was 10:30 a.m. when John took a call from Nagajima, Shin-Hifu's chief negotiator. He suggested that they meet again the next day to talk. John sighed. Of course, MTI would meet with them as requested, but his patience was worn pretty thin. The last thing he wanted was to sit through another meeting where nothing of interest happened. This time he was wrong.

John's Lessons

- Many products are made from Japanese components. Sometimes locating an attractive partner can be as simple as reviewing the list of OEM suppliers.

- In negotiations with a Japanese company, success is directly correlated with the level of preparation. The following are recommended:
    a) Thorough market research
    b) Professional preparation
    c) A detailed prospectus
    d) Regulatory approval or plan
    e) Grassroots academic support
  Be prepared to have every thing you give them checked and double-checked.

- Chances are the Japanese side will be much more patient in a negotiating setting. One reason is cultural, another is that it typically is not their technology languishing during the negotiating period. It is essential to create a strong incentive to keep things moving. The most powerful incentive is the fear of loss. Never negotiate with only a single company.

- Create a minimum set of criteria for partnering and be prepared to stick with it. Also be prepared for repeated rejections. In most cases, the Japanese have found with time and repetition, Westerners will back down and concede points.

23

John Learns About Negotiations, Japan Style

John found it fascinating that each member, including himself, sat in the same chair at every meeting. As always, the Shin-Hifu team filed in and sat around the conference table in their unofficially reserved chairs.

Bruce settled into his chair and picked slowly at his fingernails in preparation for another grilling session, identical to those of the past four months. Pleasantries were exchanged, but without the effervescence of the first meetings.

The silence was broken only by the sounds of shuffling paper which had accumulated in huge mounds on each side of the table. Finally, Nagajima broke the silence. "We understand that you are still in discussions with Chusai."

John was caught off-guard by the comment. "Of course. I thought we were perfectly clear on that fact months ago." Six sets of eyes on the other side of the table darted from side to side, a bit like crows sitting in a row on an electrical wire waiting to be zapped. The subsequent silence was unnerving. John continued. "As we have told you many, many times, we cannot break off discussions with other companies until we have a tangible gesture of good faith from Shin-Hifu."

"We are willing to sign a letter of intent," Nagajima said hopefully.

"That is an excellent start. But as we have said countless times, you must also pay a letter of intent fee. We will then negotiate exclusively with Shin-Hifu for a stipulated amount of time." John droned on from a unwritten script burned permanently into his neural pathways. What impressed John every time he repeated the statement was that the Japanese side pretended they had heard it for the very first time.

This time John did not break the silence. He was determined that Shin-Hifu would speak next.

Finally, Nagajima bobbed to the surface. "How much does MTI want for this LOI fee?"

"One million dollars," John answered tonelessly.

Shock registered on each face of the Japanese contingent, even though they had discussed this very issue in excruciating detail the week before. Shin-Hifu had re-stated their absolute policy against paying an up-front fee of any type and that an LOI fee was simply out of the question.

"That's too much." Nagajima's adam's apple started quivering noticeably, as it always did when they discussed this subject.

John continued with the well-rehearsed script. "As we have discussed, it is not so much the exact amount of one million dollars that is crucial here. Instead, it represents a commitment on the part of Shin-Hifu and without that commitment we are unwilling to break off negotiations with our other potential partners. The LOI fee together with a deadline will provide a structure for our negotiations and ensure that they do not drag on forever." While Shin-Hifu knew that MTI was still talking with Chusai, they did not seem to know that the artificial joint company was willing immediately to fork over the LOI fee. Maybe Shin-Hifu did know. But Chusai was at the bottom of his wish list and he wanted to play out Shin-Hifu to the end.

The drama continued. "We are willing to sign a letter of intent," Nagajima repeated. He appeared to have not heard a single word John said. It was simply one time too many for Bruce. He jumped to his feet, grabbed his head and ran from the room. Concerned about his friend and associate, John followed him from the room. Bruce had run to an outside balcony in the office, where he commenced to start screaming in total derangement. Seeing John, he howled miserably, "I can't take it anymore. I have to get out of here." Something had snapped inside of Bruce. He had been through the process too many times and he had finally cracked under the weight of multiple contradictions and too much *tatemae* and too little *honne*. Bruce fell to his knees, tears streaming down his cheeks and his voice alternating between sobs and cackling laughter.

The meeting adjourned to allow John, Dr. Morita and Goro to accompany Bruce to the nearby hospital where he was quickly checked into the psychiatric word. The trio watched in horror and disbelief as Bruce bounced wildly around the confines of his six-foot-by- six-foot padded cell.

John's Lessons

- Even with the best of preparations, negotiating with Japanese companies is a marathon. Positions, facts, and ideas are repeated over, over and over again in an attempt to find soft spots. This tactic has also been used countless times at the governmental level between the U.S. and Japan.

24

John's Negotiations Take a Toll

There was a deep sadness in both the JBBD and MTI offices as it became apparent that Bruce's reign as the king of biomedical consulting in Japan was over. The Japanese doctors offered little hope for a recovery. They thought he possibly could be released by mid-1999, maybe earlier, but he would require medication for the rest of his life. He had simply snapped.

Difficult as it was to deal with Bruce's collapse, the MTI team forged on with their mission. As they prepared for the next Shin-Hifu negotiating session, John decided that enough was enough. This was going to be the last session. Either Shin-Hifu agreed to the LOI fee or John would pull the plug on the negotiations. John did not want to join Bruce in his padded cell. Besides, he had another company on the line willing to pay.

Both teams soberly entered the conference room and took their seats, carefully avoiding Bruce's old chair. Dr. Morita solemnly placed a pink carnation on the table in front of his chair and observed a moment of silence. Dr. Morita was his old and trusted friend and colleague and worried deeply about Bruce. The mood was very somber.

After a brief inquiry about Bruce's condition, Nagajima began. "We are willing to sign a letter of intent for the exclusive right to negotiate on an indefinite basis."

It was too much. John shot to his feet. Everyone at the table drew back in shock and horror at the prospect of another foreigner flying berserk from the conference room. Instead, John slammed his hands down on the conference table, hard, harder than he had anticipated. Pure silence fell on the group. Dr. Morita reached for his belt for his *kendo* sword, a purely instinctive move based on a lifetime of *kendo* practice. Very slowly and with a outward calmness nearly betrayed by his total frustration, John said: "No LOI fee, no more negotiations."

The Shin-Hifu entourage sat motionless. No word passed between them. Three minutes later, a quiet but brisk discussion ensued on the Japanese side of the table. Whispers, grunts and gestures continued for several minutes. Finally, Nagajima asked to use the telephone. John motioned for him to use the phone in his office where he could speak privately. The MTI side sat silent, unwilling to break their vow to avenge Bruce's breakdown.

Nagajima returned to the room and spoke briefly with his team. They stopped. Nagajima looked in John's direction and said, "Five-hundred thousand dollars."

John looked at the ceiling for a few moments, thought of Bruce and counted to ten. He suddenly stuck out his hand in agreement.

The LOI took two months to draft. but seven months into the ordeal, the money was paid to the MTI account and the other two companies were told that discussions were terminated.

John's Lessons

- Japanese corporate warriors are extremely risk adverse. They have little incentive to take risks since mistakes are punished so severely. But when a corporate decision has been made to solidify a deal and there is a real threat that the warriors may return home empty handed, a different kind of risk comes into play. This also becomes a risk of possible failure. When the failure risk quotient is balanced with the financial risk quotient they have no choice but to make the supreme leap of faith and reach into their wallets.

25

The Saga of John's Negotiations Continues

With the LOI signed and the fee paid, the intensity of the negotiations grew in direct proportion to the approach of the negotiation deadline. Although a piddling sum for a company the size of Shin-Hifu, the LOI fee represented a huge shift in the balance of power in favor of MTI.

Still, the level of negotiated detail assumed awesome proportions. By the time the proposed agreement reached the third draft and was well over a hundred pages long, John was beginning to look favorably on Bruce's new accomodations. It was decided that the up-front fee would be paid in the form of an advance purchase of product and that a guaranteed sales forecast would be incorporated. But the actual numbers were always left conspicuously blank and carefully avoided. Both sides seemed unwilling to confront this "minor" issue until the very end. While they had been discussed ad nauseam informally over lakes of alcohol, no official number had been offered or given. Hundreds of pages of spreadsheets were prepared, countered, and re-proposed. But the moment of truth had drawn very close.

The decisive meeting was scheduled to be held at the MTI headquarters in L.A.

"We cannot pay any money until we have actual orders from customers," Nagajima said with a straight face. Big Ed was participating in these final discussions. "What the fuck did he say?" Big Ed looked accusingly at John.

John's heart stopped in midbeat at this newest gambit. He had expected a lively "how much and when" debate from the Shin-Hifu team. But this was beyond comprehension. A zero-figure was never even a remote possibility. In fact, agreement on an up-front payment was written into the LOI. That LOI was fast approaching expiration, with only three weeks before Shin-Hifu forfeited their exclusive negotiation fee. John never doubted their good faith willingness to negotiate.

Until now, that is. John pulled away from Big Ed's glare and stammered, "But you've already agreed to the payment. We're here to discuss how much and when you will take product delivery."

"We never said that," Nagajima delivered back in complete innocence.

Enlightenment hit John like a sandbag. They were serious. John immediately called a meeting for the MTI team in Big Ed's private office overlooking the haze of west L.A. He listened to Big Ed's expletives, none deleted, for about five minutes. Once the initial assault was weathered, John moved the discussions onto a rational plane. The MTI team collectively came to the realization that the negotiations were over. In the grand scheme of things, the LOI fee itself was insignificant compared to their possible loss here. As disappointing as it was to let go now, they would simply have to let go of Shin-Hifu and return to their other prospective partners. But John was angry about the entire process. Despite the grinding quality of the process, he had come to respect and even like the members of the Shin-Hifu team. He had looked forward to working shoulder to shoulder with them to build the Japan business after the contract was finally signed. Now everything was ashes. There was no way they could back down on their demands. The idea that they would enter into a long-term, exclusive contract without up-front fees or guaranteed minimum sales was pure insanity.

The MTI team returned to the conference room, minus Big Ed who simply disappeared on some kind of errand he said. Their heads were bowed. After nearly a year of marathon meetings, the group was crushed by the disappointment of it all. John moved to English and spoke for the group. "Well, I guess we are stuck then. Perhaps we should all just pack it in."

The Shin-Hifu team quickly exchanged glances, trying to confirm the exact meaning of the American colloquialisms. Nagajima stepped in. "What about the deadline? What about our exclusive negotiating fee?" he said accusingly.

"I'm sorry, we haven't even discussed that," John replied wearily. "I suppose we can get back to you on that after we discuss it. For now, the only thing we can say is that without the fees that were clearly agreed to in the LOI, we are stuck." John lapsed into silence. No one else spoke. Finally, John remembered that they had reserved a room at an exclusive restaurant in Beverly Hills, where he had thought they would celebrate the consummation of their deal. Now, it seemed like a pretty bad idea. With no enthusiasm, John asked them, "I don't see any purpose really, but if you want, we can still meet for dinner tonight."

The Shin-Hifu team huddled and after an extended discussion said they wanted to meet for dinner anyway. They looked equally unenthusiastic about the prospect of a social gathering with their erstwhile ex-partner. After the Shin-Hifu team returned to their hotel, John walked out of the MTI building and over to a sparsely wooded area. There, he tried to destroy a medium-sized birch tree with his bare hands.

To everyone's regret, Big Ed joined them for the dinner at the fancy Beverly Hills restaurant. Maybe it was the prospect of seeing a new starlet or maybe it was the free meal on the company tab. In any event, the MTI team arrived ten minutes late because they had to stop off at the emergency room of Santa Monica Hospital to have John's hand stitched up after his little tantrum in the wilds of Santa Monica.

The two teams hardly exchanged pleasantries. As John sat down, gingerly holding his hand above the table, the person he felt truly sorry for was Bruce. He knew that Bruce needed the eight percent finder's fee for engineering the deal for his mounting hospital bills. Oh well.

After a few words of small talk, Nagajima cleared his throat. "I think there may have been some misunderstanding."

"Oh," John responded with the briefest flicker of hope.

"We never said that we would not pay. We said that it would be difficult to pay."

"Oh," John responded a notch higher on the hope scale.

"Japanese is such a difficult and ambiguous language," Nagajima offered.

"So, you will pay as agreed then?" John asked, excitedly translating this new development to the other MTI executives at the table.

"Of course. But we need to discuss the amount and the timing." With that, Nagajima raised his glass for a toast.

"*Kampai,*" they all said in unison.

The negotiation deadline for signing the agreement was extended and a final agreement between MTI and Shin-Hifu was finally signed three months later. MTI netted eight million dollars in the first year and obtained an aggressive but flexible guaranteed sales forecast. Big Ed, was so happy about it all, he allowed John to keep half of the money to fund the MTI Japan infrastructure.

With the contract completed, John's next order of business was to establish a fund for Bruce's hospital expenses. Bruce had graduated from the padded room and was now taking advanced courses in finger painting in the communal recreation hall. His doctors had even allowed him to use a Sony Walkman and a single Doors tape, which he listened to over and over again while fingerpainting with an intensity rarely demonstrated by a mental patient. The doctors wanted to study his brain, but John would hear none of it.

Because of the careful preparations and the comprehensive infrastructure that was put into place, the relationship with Shin-Hifu flourished. The effect was felt worldwide. Joint sales and marketing plans, service and there were even a joint development project that resulted in changes to MTI's products worldwide. Two years after the completion of the original agreement, sales had jumped to over $30 million. Flushed with success, John proposed a joint venture whereby MTI would hold a forty-percent share and an option to purchase an additional twenty percent in three years. After a $50 million payment to Shin-Hifu, Nagajima was promoted to executive vice president and a seat on the board of directors of the new JV.

By the tenth anniversary of John's arrival in Japan, MTI Japan's annual sales exceeded one hundred million U.S. dollars. On the home front, John was married to a beautiful Thai woman who was trying hard to learn English.

Life was good.

That is, until John woke from his nightmare and remembered his meeting at the MTI headquarters with Big Ed and Karen.

26

John's Daydream Is Over: Back to the Present

Seated on the limousine bus returning from Narita to the Tokyo City Air Terminal, John's dark mood was impervious to the blue skies and sunshine of the late afternoon. John knew that he would have no trouble finding another job. After his experience in building MTI Japan, he knew that he was a valuable commodity. He had also set aside a fair amount of money during his ten years, especially after recovering from Hitomi's attack on his bank accounts. He also had his stock options.

No, he wanted something else. Something new and challenging after the devastation of working for a large company, only to be betrayed in his moment of triumph. Maybe he would take his wife of nine months and return to Thailand for a bit of rest and relaxation while he contemplated his options.

But when John walked into his apartment, he realized how much he would miss this place and the work he had done. The place seemed strangely quiet. Where was his wife? For no reason at all, he recalled Hitomi and the Jamaican duo. Surely, lightning couldn't strike twice. Could it?

He also noticed the light on the answering machine flashing vigorously. He reluctantly pushed the button to receive what he was sure to be unwanted messages.

"John, Ed here. Call me." Beep.

"John, come on, call me at home." Beep. Big Ed again.

"Goddammit. Call me, you son-of-a-bitch." Beep.

"Don't be so sensitive, we need to talk." Beep.

"Please don't do this to me. No hard feelings, OK?" Beep.

Big Ed obviously thought the trip across the Pacific only took a few hours. Glancing at his watch, John noticed that it was 3:00 a.m. in L.A. He thought, what the hell, and picked up the phone. After a few rings he heard a gruff, "Who the hell do you think you are calling at this hour?"

"Ed, John here. You asked me to call."

"Johnny boy! Damn glad you called. Been worried sick. About that little misunderstanding we had yesterday. . . ."

John cut him short. "What about Karen?" he asked pointedly.

"Amazing thing there. It turns out, she's been boinking Knowland for the last couple years. Boinked a few others, too. Patrick in personnel, Don in procurement, and even ole Mitchell in sales. Anyway. It turns out that Knowland had really taken a liking to her and told his wife number four that the gig was up. Then, he finds out that she's splitting to the Land of the Rising Sun. Patrick was pretty broken about it all and decided to file a sexual harassment suit. When Knowland found out about it and checked everything out and he discovered that not only was the lovely Karen boinking everybody on the twenty-sixth floor, but the janitor in the basement, too. Hey, John wait a second."

John waited for a couple minutes, listening to Big Ed spew expletives. Then he heard the sounds of shuffling paper. Finally, Big Ed came back on the phone.

"Goddamn, goddamn, goddamn," Ed repeated this at least another dozen times.

"What is it?" John asked, sensing that the entire organization was being ripped apart by the exploding scandal.

"Goddamn," Big Ed repeated. "I don't know which is more amazing, the fact that she was screwing the janitor and he is filing a sexual harassment case against MTI, or the fact that she is filing a sexual harassment case against me. Can you imagine such a thing? Against me?"

"You boinked her didn't you, Ed?" John said with a barely suppressed giggle, envisioning a swarm of lawyers circling as the entire

MTI executive staff filed a sexual harassment suit against the company and each other.

"All right, all right. I admit it. I did. But I was drunk the first time, so that doesn't count? Right? I mean, come on. You understand, don't you?"

Unable to control himself any longer, John burst out in laughter. John hung up on Big Ed, happy to be free at last.

Three Years Later...

John was sitting at his large desk in front of the window when his secretary buzzed him and told him he had a call from a Dr. Knowland at the Hotel Okura in downtown Tokyo.

"Jack—Hello," he answered amiably.

MTI was now John's second largest client. After the huge scandal erupted at MTI three years earlier, John had decided it was better to hunker down for awhile. Jack Knowland had waved plenty of cash and perks in front of John to get him to come back from being fired by Big Ed. Dr. Knowland roused himself from retirement to save from disintegration the company he had founded. But John just waved good-bye. Several months after that fateful trip to L.A., John bought JBBD from Bruce and moved into the Japan biomedical consulting business. His jump to consulting coincided with a pretty sharp recession and the bulk of JBBD's clients headed for the hills, leaving John receptive to Knowland's repeated offers to help MTI Japan.

Now, JBBD was thriving due to a combination of John's hard work and the reflected glory of Bruce's past achievements. Based on his own experience, John preached a never-ceasing gospel of take control to his foreign clients. He encouraged them to play the game according to local rules and did his best to help them level the playing field.

As for MTI, well, a total of twenty-one sexual harassment suits were filed in a single day at the Santa Monica Municipal Court House. It was a record for corporate America, according to a multipart *Wall Street Journal* report.

Dr. Knowland was forced to take back day-to-day control of the company. He married the stunning Karen to avoid a twenty-second harassment suit. The marriage lasted thirteen months and sixteen days and ended in the cremation of most of Knowland's assets. Karen now lives in Beverly Hills in Knowland's former mansion. Knowland was off the talk show circuit.

Big Ed dropped off the corporate screen, but recent sightings placed him in San Diego as a short order cook at a Denny's near the airport.

"John, would you please have someone pick me up at the hotel for our meeting? The taxi line is always a mile long and I don't want to be late for our meeting."

"I'll send my driver right over," John promised.

John pushed a button on his desk. "Bruce. Please pick up Dr. Knowland in front of the Hotel Okura. And, don't forget to wash your hands!"

John's Lessons

- While the path to success in Japan is seldom easy or strewn with rose petals, the fact is that many such companies have achieved success in the Japanese market.

- For the Westerner who heads a foreign company in Japan, success can be within his or her grasp with patience, understanding, committment, focus, and, of course, good technology.

- Although very intangible, we feel that perhaps the key ingredient for success in Japan (and the one most often left out of the recipe) is *passion*. To be successful in Japan, to endure the slings and arrows of outrageous fortune, to stand on the top of the mountain and survey all below, a Western manager must have a passion for achieving success in Japan.

About the Authors

Mark A. Colby
Mr. Colby graduated from Eastern Washington State University and trained in dentistry at the University of Washington. After working in sales and management for the Diagnostics Division of Abbott Laboratories, he founded Colby Group International in 1990. He now serves as vice-chairman of the American Chamber of Commerce subcommittee on medical supplies and chairs the *in vitro* diagnostics committee. He lives in Tokyo with his wife and two daughters.

Michael P. Birt, Ph.D.
Dr. Birt received his Ph.D. in Japanese Studies from Princeton. Prior to joining CGI as a corporate co-founder in 1992, he consulted in Japan for many of the world's leading multinational companies. He is a member of the Advisory Council for East Asian Studies at Princeton University and now lives in Seattle where he manages the U.S. office of CGI. He is married with two daughters.